IB

English A: Language and Literature

Revision Guide

Fiona Swanson

Acknowledgements

Colleagues, students, family and friends have all made contributions to this guide that deserve acknowledgement, whether for their lively conversation, their professional support, their willingness to trial materials and share their work, or their patience and understanding.

I have benefitted particularly from the clear critical thinking and advice of my friend and colleague Jo Sale, Head of Sixth Form and IB Coordinator at Impington International Sixth Form, Cambridge; and from the patient, thoughtful and thorough proofreading of Miranda Swanson.

Most significant of all is Mary Robbins, who has given me practical advice and guidance throughout the writing process; it could not have been completed without her professional editorial skills and publishing experience, her patience, and the countless hours of her time she gave so willingly.

Contents

Chapter Three   **46**

Chapter Four

Chapter Five

Considering poetry

Chapter One

The purpose of this book

This revision guide prepares you for the different assessment areas of the English A: Language and Literature course. It summarises and explains these assessment elements, and reviews the analytical skills you have acquired during the course.

To be fully prepared for your exams and other assessments, you need to understand the ideas the course is based on, so every section of this book includes relevant discussion of these ideas, explaining how they relate to the different assessment areas. Unlike the revision guide for a content based subject, this guide does not revise texts you have studied – that would be impossible, because the range from which a school selects its texts is so great that no two will select the same ones. This guide, therefore, focuses on the skills you have developed and the understanding you have gained of the ways language conveys meaning, rather than on revisiting individual texts. It deals with the written tasks and oral assessments as well as the two examination papers, since these are all part of your formal assessment – its purpose is to prepare you for the entirety of your assessment and not just for your written exams.

The contents pages are detailed, so you can look up particular points as you need to; and at the end there is a glossary of terms you will find useful when you analyse or comment on literary and non-literary texts. You will find that just reading it through is a good revision exercise, since the words in it will recall the different parts of the course you have studied. There is also an appendix where there are Paper One practice exam papers for standard and higher levels.

Notes

- The detail of the assessments, the criteria and the level descriptors are to be found in the IB guide to the course, a document you will have had access to throughout the course – you should make sure you are familiar with it.

- This is not a course or study guide; the purpose of such a guide is to help you to understand the course as you study it. The focus here is on helping you to prepare for the assessed activities, written and oral.

The English A: Language and Literature course

What is this course really about?

It is about how we communicate meaning, why, and with whom. It is about the things that influence the way we communicate, like who we're talking to, or what our situation, or context, is; that is, all the influences on how a text is produced. It is also about all the influences on how it is understood: the reader has a context that influences the way s/he understands a text as well. You may have seen this when reading a text in translation – if it comes, as it should for this course, from a culture with which you are not familiar, it may seem strange or difficult. It obviously wouldn't to people in the country or culture it comes from, so you can see that your understanding is influenced by what you bring to the text yourself. If it seems strange, that strangeness comes from you and not the text, and developing your wider cultural understanding is a key element in the course. It is precisely because of this that the requirement is there: true to the IB aim that its graduates should be global in their outlook and understanding.

What is meant by the term "text"?

For this course, the word "text" is used to refer to the widest possible range of ways people convey meaning, or communicate: orally, in writing, and visually. This includes literary and non-literary written texts, but also such media items as film, television, and radio; and the wide and increasing range of electronic "new media" texts like blogs, websites, and tweets. It also includes visual images with or without words, like cartoons, advertisements, or paintings.

How is this reflected in the specific aims of the course?

The course aims can be summarised in the following points:

- to introduce you to texts of all sorts, written in different periods and places, and arising from different cultures – that is, to different text types and contexts

- to help you to understand and appreciate how the context in which a text is produced affects its meaning, whether historical, social, political or cultural

- to enable you to gain an understanding of other cultures through their texts, and an awareness and enjoyment of their different perspectives

- to develop your ability to consider the relationship between writer, text, audience and purpose and to understand that the text results from the interaction between author, purpose and audience

- to develop your ability to produce detailed, close analysis of all types of text, both orally and in writing

- to enhance your ability to express your views, ideas and responses fully and clearly, both orally and in writing and in a variety of different ways

- to help you to understand and appreciate the presentational and stylistic conventions that characterise different texts, and their aesthetic effect

Will I have to use English perfectly?

No. (Does anyone?) This is not a second language course, and it assumes a high level of fluency and understanding from the outset; but neither is it exclusively for "mother tongue" users of English. It is for students, of whom there are many studying for the IB Diploma, for whom English is their working language, or one of two languages (or more!) spoken equally well. So while there will be some whose "mother tongue" is English, there will be others as well. You are expected to be able to use a broad and precise vocabulary, with accurate grammar and sentencing, to express nuances of meaning in the consideration of complex ideas. Perfection is not required!

How will I be assessed?

This will be explained in detail in the relevant sections of the revision guide, but in brief you will have two written exams, and you will be required to produce written coursework in the form of written tasks. These are assessed externally. Your oral work will be assessed internally, within your school; there are two aspects to this: one is the Individual Oral Commentary (IOC) – this is recorded, marked by your teacher, and sent to an external examiner for moderation. The other is the Further Oral Activities (FOAs).

How does the course content fit the assessment elements?

The table in the next section illustrates the connection between what you learn during the course and how you will be assessed; or, to put it another way, it shows how the course prepares you for the assessments.

Does each different part of the course prepare me for a different part of the assessment?

Yes and no. Again, the table clarifies this, as will the relevant sections of the guide. But for Paper One, for instance, a text analysis exam, all four parts of the course go towards your exam preparation, and they are equally important; on the other hand, Paper Two refers to the literary texts you have read for part three, and the IOC is based on the literary texts you have read in part four of the course. The FOAs arise from parts one and two, and the Written Tasks arise from all four parts.

Overview of Course Structure

Before you start preparing for the different assessment tasks, it may be useful to remind yourself what the course looks like overall, and where the assessment components fit in.

In the following plan, the first two columns show how each part of the course is assessed. The third column shows how the texts studied arise from the choice of topic, enabling you to develop the skills required for this course and meet the assessment objectives. Column three is an example, so you can see how the many texts you have read and activities you have engaged in fit into the assessment framework. Schools choose their own topics and texts within the framework of the English A: Language and Literature course guide, and select most of their literary texts from the two IB set booklists: the Prescribed List of Authors (PLA) and the Prescribed Literature in Translation (PLT). The texts you have studied will be different from the ones in this table, but this example shows what a typical course looks like.

In the chapters that follow, each assessment component is addressed separately, so that you understand what it requires, how it relates to the course content, and how you can prepare for it.

Syllabus Component	Assessment Component	Example of Course Content

Part 1:
 	
Language in Cultural Context
	Paper 1
	
	Written Task
	
	Further Oral Activity
		Examples of Topics: Conflict
		                             Prejudice
		                             Language Change
		
		• texts relating to language/dialects dying out. For example Cromarty
		• implications of the imposition of colonial languages on formerly colonised countries, for example India or Rwanda
		• language and identity, for example South Africa under Apartheid
		• implications on language use arising from new communication technologies, for example text messaging
		• political speeches, for example President Obama's acceptance speech; Martin Luther King's "I have a dream..."
		• language change in the USA according to ethnic demographic
		• acceptance of and provision for languages of minority ethnic groups in the UK, for example Urdu or Hindi
		• politicians' speeches at time of atomic attack on Hiroshima

Syllabus Component	Assessment Component	Example of Course Content This example is for higher level; where the requirements for standard level are different there is an indicating note

Part 2:
 	
Language and Mass Communication
	Paper 1
	
	Written Task
	
	Further Oral Activity
		Topics: Conflict
		    Prejudice
		    Media Language
		
		• comparison of advertising for regular coffee and fairly traded coffee
		• language of advertising – developments in style and approach, for example "anti-advertising" as a campaign tool
		• campaigns and language of persuasion, for example: Amnesty International campaign to stop violence against women
		• importance of audience, for example Kony documentary
		• Stephen Lawrence – media coverage at the time of his murder; the MacPherson Report; coverage of the 2012 trial of his murderers
		• comparison of media texts at the time of the atomic attack on Hiroshima

Part 3: Literature – texts and contexts	**Paper 2** **Written Task**	**Literary texts:** • Play: I Will Marry When I Want; Ngugi Wa Thiongo • Play: Othello; William Shakespeare • Novel: Lord of the Flies Note: At standard level only two works are studied
Part 4: Literature – Critical Study	Individual Oral Commentary (IOC) Written Task	**Literary texts:** • Play: Sizwe Bansi is Dead; Athol Fugard • Novel: Animal Farm; George Orwell • Poetry: Wilfred Owen Note: At standard level only two works are studied

This choice of texts shows how parts 3 and 4 can be studied within the same broad topics. This example uses the broad topics of **conflict** and **prejudice** in Part One and Two; the texts for Parts Three and Four fit within these topics.

Chapter Two

External Assessment: Exam Paper One – The analysis essay

Introduction

As you can see from the chart in Chapter One, Paper One is a written examination worth 25% of your final grade. It tests your skills in textual analysis, and the entire course prepares you for it.

You are likely to have studied some literary texts in the past, before you started this course, and you may have learned about some aspects of the media; you are less likely to have studied individual media texts in the same way as you have approached literary texts. You may not have had an opportunity to engage in the detailed analysis of specific text extracts, whether non-literary or literary.

Success in this exam depends on your ability not only to understand how language is used to achieve its purpose within its context, but also to be able to describe this in detail and specifically, in an organised and coherent way. You will need to be able to use accurately a range of technical terms in order to write a detailed analysis and avoid generalisations. There is a list of such terms at the end of the guide – *the glossary of terms for text analysis* – and while you don't need to be able to use all of them, so there is no need to learn them by heart, reading through the list and referring to it will certainly help you to understand how you can write a more focused analysis.

There is no optimum plan for a text analysis essay; some approaches will follow from the extracts themselves, and depending on your response to the extracts you will engage in different ways. Nevertheless, there are aspects of any text that you need to consider: questions about purpose and context, recognition and identification of stylistic features, understanding of the use of formal features of language and how they may differ according to text type and audience. The samples included in this chapter will help you to understand how to organise your ideas to write an effective analysis essay.

What does the exam consist of?

Paper One tests your analytical skills by giving you short texts or extracts you have not seen before, and asking you to analyse them. The assessment criteria help you to understand what is being asked of you as much as the instruction at the beginning of the paper, and you should be thoroughly familiar with them. For Paper One there are four criteria, testing your understanding of and response to the texts, the organisation of your essay, and the clarity and accuracy of your language.

Outline of assessment criteria at standard level

If you are taking the course at standard level, your examination paper will contain two extracts, taken from a very broad range of text types, and completely different from each other. You will be required to select one of them. Your analysis should include comment on the significance of context and purpose, and take into account formal and stylistic features.

The four assessment criteria look for the following:

- Understanding of the text – this includes understanding its context and purpose as well as the text type; you are expected to illustrate your comments with specific references to the text.

- Understanding of how the stylistic features of the text – including its use of language, its tone, the writer's style, and structure – are used to create its meaning; and what effect they have on the audience.

- How organised and coherent your essay is, and how logically you have presented your ideas.

- How accurately you use language, how varied your vocabulary and use of technical terminology, and how appropriate are your register and style.

Outline of assessment criteria at higher level

If you are taking the course at higher level, your examination paper will contain two pairs of passages, and you will be required to choose one pair. While they will be different text types, they will share some aspect of content – both could address holidays, for instance, but one may be the text of a talk about the damage our holiday habit has on the environment, while the other may be an advertisement for a cruise. You will be asked to include comments in your answer on the similarities and differences between them and their approach to their subject. You will also comment on the significance of context and purpose, and the use of formal and stylistic features.

The four assessment criteria look for the following:

- Understanding and comparison of the texts – this includes how well you understand the two texts and can identify their type, purpose, audience, and contexts; how well you understand the differences and similarities between them (point of view is one aspect of this, but use of language is another); and how well you support your analysis by making specific and detailed reference to the texts.

- Understanding of how stylistic features are used and what effect they have – this means how well you demonstrate your understanding of how the meaning of a text is conveyed through choice of stylistic features; and what effect these have on the reader.

- How organised and coherent your essay is, to what extent you have addressed the texts equally in a structured comparative analysis essay.

- Language – how clearly and accurately you use language; how appropriate your style is, and how effectively you use a broad range of analytical terminology to convey your meaning precisely.

The four parts of the course

The course is designed to prepare you to meet these criteria in a variety of ways, and later in this chapter there is an outline of how all the four parts of the course contribute to your development of the necessary skills.

Before that we take a detailed critical look at the language of persuasion and practical guidance on how to analyse various persuasive media texts. Paper One may well include texts from literary sources, so following this focus on non-literary texts there is a section addressing the analysis of texts of a literary nature. This section shows that we cannot compartmentalise language, as though poetry had its own language and stylistic features while advertising had another; poetry frequently aims to persuade, for instance, and advertisements frequently use imagery, rhythm and rhyme.

As we have already seen, the Language A: Language and Literature course thinks of language as the means by which human beings communicate, differently according to the context, language user, audience and purpose; and changing in response to those same factors.

The division into four parts highlights differences of focus in the way language is used. It ensures that attention is given equally to what we think of as literature and all the other ways we use language. It should help you to understand that the technical and stylistic features of language you are addressing in your analysis are the same whatever the text type. They can be, and are, used differently, but there is not a separate chunk for literature, for instance, or for media, or for political campaigns, or anything else. So a ballad may use repetition for emphasis, but so may a politician's rhetorical speech; a poem and an advertisement may both use rhyme and rhythm; a journalist's prose is likely to make use of imagery just as a novelist's is. We only have the stylistic features that exist in the language, whatever our purpose and however we use them.

What we can say, however, is that different text types may make more use of some stylistic features than others – a ballad is likely to use repetition more systematically, and more often, than a politician's speech; an advertisement is likely to use rhythm and rhyme in an obvious way so we remember the product when we see it in the shops, while a poem will usually use it much more subtly.

Some people say they find poetry harder to analyse than prose, and some people say they find non-literary texts harder. If you share either of these views, it should help you to realise that actually you are looking for the same stylistic features, whatever the text, used sometimes for different reasons and in different ways.

The four parts of the course all address the analytical reading of texts, with an emphasis on non-literary text types in Parts One and Two, and the study of literary text types, genres, in Parts Three and Four. The following overview shows how this works, and links the content of all four parts of the course to the assessment criteria for Paper One.

The Language of Persuasion

Persuasion is part of everyday life for most people; either we want or need to persuade other people of something, or someone wants or needs to persuade us. Persuasion takes many forms, of course, and happens for many different reasons: it can be innocent or sinister, commercial or ethical, subtle or obvious. It can be the tool of politicians, saints, industrialists, teachers, campaigners, dictators, parents, children, doctors – it can save or spoil lives. There are many ways of persuading, and this course explores the way language is used to persuade.

In Paper One you might well be asked to analyse a persuasive text, so you need to be aware of the most important features of the language of persuasion. The following section suggests an approach to the analysis of advertisements.

The Benetton approach to advertising

Benetton provides an interesting example of how styles change and new approaches to advertising are devised so that companies can stay ahead of the game. A proudly global company, Benetton has always celebrated diversity, originally by using adult and child models from many different countries and cultures to advertise their upmarket clothing ranges. In recent years, the Benetton brand has been promoted not by creating heart-warming, happy pictures of people from all over the world wearing beautiful Benetton clothes; it has adopted a much more adventurous approach to keeping its name in the public eye. Maintaining its distinguishing global ethos, it has attached its name to social concerns that go beyond national boundaries. For example, it had one campaign that famously challenged racism and celebrated multiculturalism, and another that aimed to raise awareness about HIV/AIDS. Sometimes they shock; this still makes people remember the name. The effect has been to associate Benetton with important issues as an active agent for change.

The two advertisements seen here are recent examples of this strategy, taking it further.

The first thing you notice is that they are identical in almost every way. Similarities are:

- The banner headline

- The Benetton logo

- The same text beneath with statistical information about unemployed young people

- The same information about a competition for unemployed young people

- The same invitation to participate in it

- The young people are in the same pose, looking at the same thing

- The same sense of things being wrong socially

- Exactly the same design, clothes, plain background

The only differences are:

- Different young people

- Different text describing them, in small print, making it clear that they are real people and not models

- They come from different countries, showing that the problem is global – as is the solution: Benetton!

- The target audience is referred to a website to get further involved in this feel-good campaign. This shows that the advertisements are part of a multi-media endeavour which is evidently global. Think carefully about who the target audience might be: clearly global, young, and in spite of the focus on unemployment, not poor.

- You will be able to identify more features to comment on, like the witty invention of words – *unemployee* and *unhate* – which lightens the otherwise sombre mood. These two advertisements illustrate the link between advertising and the society it targets. They also show that advertising must be creative and imaginative if it is to persuade its target audience successfully.

"What's in a word?" – advertisements and persuasion

Some background to analytical details

Advertisements are fun to analyse! Many other text types use language persuasively, but no others are as unambiguous in their purpose. Their aim is to sell something; this might be something material, or it could be an idea, a political party, an event, or an action. Here we are using advertisements for commercial products as the most direct example of the use of the language of persuasion.

In your analysis you will work out who an advertisement is intended to sell the product to, and how it uses language and visual images persuasively to do so. If you look at advertisements or television commercials from previous decades, you will see that fifty years ago they were very direct – they more or less simply said "Buy me!" With the passage of time they have become more subtle, less direct and more varied in the way they engage their target audience. Sometimes they don't allude to the product they are advertising at all, as you can see in many recent adverts for United Colors of Benetton, the well known European clothes company. The target audience only knows the advertisement is for clothing because they recognise the brand name, which is included somewhere in the picture. If you do not recognise the brand name, you might think these advertisements are about social injustices. The sample from a very recent Benetton campaign shows how sophisticated advertising methods have become compared with the naive seeming simple approach of earlier years.

The positioning of an advertisement also has a significant influence on the language and images used, which is something you may need to take into account when planning written tasks. You will certainly consider it for Paper One.

A useful way to approach the analysis of any advertisement is to ask lots of questions about it – your answers will form the basis of your analysis. You can practise doing this with any advertisement; look at it carefully, noting in detail who the people are in it; how the text is written; how it is presented visually using technical codes; what product it is selling; whether it makes allusions to people, events or objects outside its framework; whether it is funny, serious, informative. The more questions you ask, the more effectively you will be able to write a detailed analysis.

When you look at advertisements from even the quite recent past, you will realise that they become dated rather quickly. This is because advertising is very immediate, designed to succeed quickly in the consumer society we live in – you will have heard the saying that yesterday's advertisements are no more relevant than yesterday's news. Adverts therefore reflect society's ideas, its hopes and fears, trends in humour and music; and its stereotypes and prejudices. This is why they quickly lose impact – it is important to understand this, because addressing context is part of your analysis. So, if you were to analyse an advertisement for detergent made in the 1950s, it would almost certainly feature a woman as a stereotypical housewife, doing her best to ensure that her husband and children are super clean – white shirts glowing while Mrs Next Door's family's clothes are greyish in comparison! Much use is made of stereotypes in advertising, of gender, race, social class, nationality, childhood and other groups, and in your analysis you will reflect on how a particular stereotype makes the advertisement more persuasive. You might want to comment on how stereotypes have changed, and link that to changes in social equality. It would be a mistake to imagine that advertisements exist in a bubble, independent of their social and political context, even if what they are doing is selling detergent; they will still reflect the society and values of their time.

Analysis

Basically, when analysing an advertisement you are answering the question. "How does it work?" Advertising is a huge part of a marketing budget, and is supported by research into the appropriate demographic to ensure that it is effective, that the money spent is not wasted, and that the people who are targeted do buy the product. This is true not only for the commercial world of material products, but also for the world of ideas – political, ethical, and social. You only have to think of any political election campaign to see this. Presidents and prime ministers engage advertising consultants to "sell" them to the voting public.

The following questions look at specific aspects of an advertisement in order to answer the question "How does it work?" The questions are grouped in categories; you could apply them to television commercials as well as to printed advertisements; your analysis essay could be organised according to these sections. Try taking any advertisement and asking these questions: the more you practise, the easier it will become.

Representation of people

- Are they old or young?

- Are they male or female?

- What ethnic group do they belong to?

- Do they belong to an identifiable social group? How do you know?

- What sort of clothes are they wearing?

- What can you tell from their facial expressions?

- What can you tell from their body language?

- Are there any obvious stereotypes? What are they?

- How do the people in the advertisement relate to each other?

Your answers to these questions will help you to work out who the advertiser is targeting specifically and who is being excluded. The link between advertising and social norms, conventions and ideas will be easier to identify.

Presentation/Format

- What can you work out from the positioning of images in the foreground or background?

- What use is made of perspective?

- Are there any omissions? Has anything been left out of the picture? Why?

- If the advert is photographic, how have the people been arranged in relation to each other, and to any other objects in the picture?

- Is there anything significant about the lighting?

- What does the use of colour or black and white indicate?

- If the image is not photographic, what is its style? (Is it a cartoon, for instance, or a reproduction of a well known artistic masterpiece?) Why is this chosen?

- What is the setting of the advert? Why?

- Does the item being advertised appear in the advert? If it doesn't, why doesn't it?

Use of text

- How do the words work with the images, adding to or clarifying the message?

- Who is the advertisement talking to? Who is speaking?

- Is there anything else in the advertisement that helps to explain the images?

- How would you describe the page layout – typeface, font size, technical aspects of presentation?

The advertisement overall

- Does the advert allude to external events? (For instance, in a period of economic recession, to financial hardship?)

- Does it allude to other advertisements or products?

- Is there a story? What is it?

- Do we identify with anyone in the advert? Who? Why?

- Is there an assumption of shared ideas, that some things are universally desirable or undesirable? That some people will naturally have certain roles?

- Does the advertisement make any claims or promises? Are these realistic?

The wider context

Your answers to the questions above will help you to address the advertisement as a whole.

- Who is the target audience of the advert, and how do you know?

- Where is the advertisement likely to appear? Not just "in a newspaper", but which one? Be specific. What makes you think this?

- Do you need any knowledge of facts or events outside of the advertisement in order to fully understand it? What does this tell you about the product being advertised, or about its context?

- Can you tell or do you know if the advert is part of a larger advertising campaign? (Advertising campaigns sometimes include television commercials and flat advertisements as part of a season's advertising, for instance.) If so, what part does it play overall?

- Is there any difference between what the advert seems to be selling and what it is really selling? An advert for detergent, for instance, wants us to buy the detergent itself, but the advertisement may well be actually pretending that by buying this product you are being a good mother. Sometimes adverts sell a product by selling a desirable idea.

Try working through these questions on a variety of types of advertisement for a range of products. You may see a connection between the kind of product being advertised and the method of advertising it; compare adverts for regular instant coffee with those promoting fairly traded coffee, for instance. Do you detect a difference of values? Where and how do you see this?

Engaging with advertisements, understanding how they are designed to function in relation to their target audience and their context, and how the language they use changes accordingly, will help you to understand and write about any persuasive text: written or spoken texts of politicians, campaigns for humanitarian action, charitable drives to raise funds for a worthy cause – all these and many more will use persuasive language devices and stylistic features to ensure that they are successful in engaging their target audience. Language is used to persuade for good ends as well as bad – fully informed about how language and images have been used to persuade, you can choose what you buy – or buy into!

Persuasive features in campaigns

The questions above would be as relevant if you were analysing campaign materials for humanitarian, charitable or ethical causes as they are for the analysis of commercial advertisements. If the exam included an awareness raising poster, or a charitable appeal, for example, you would approach it in the same way; change the word *advert* in the questions above to *poster* or *appeal* and try it – you will find appropriate material on the websites of any major organisation like Amnesty International, Greenpeace, Oxfam, UNICEF and many others. If the text is for a humanitarian or other ethical cause or organisation, you will be looking specifically for appeals to the better side of human nature, and maybe information or graphics that would shock, sadden or frighten the target audience; often an emotional appeal.

Political campaign materials work in exactly the same way; they too will select issues and approaches that are designed to make their policies attractive to the voting public. In other words, the "product" they are persuading people to "buy" is a politician or a political party. Use the questions to show how they work, in the same way as for commercial advertisements and campaign texts.

The secret of success lies in the detail; the more you generalise, the weaker your essay will be. On the other hand, the more detailed and specific you are, the stronger your essay will be. Remember that the details are not accidental – whoever designed the text put them there for a reason.

How do I analyse a literary text?

Paper One requires you to analyse texts you have not seen before. These will come from a wide variety of sources, and could include any literary genre as well as any non literary text type. Close comment on a short extract from one of your Part Four works will be the focus of your Individual Oral Commentary, but if Paper One includes a literary extract, you may choose to analyse it. The following guidance looks particularly at the ways of writing that tend to characterise literary texts.

TS Eliot once said "It is the mark of great poetry that it often communicates before it is fully understood." The same could be said of Paper One – you will be able to say a lot about your passage even if you do not fully understand it. You will find that as you explore the way language is used, your understanding of the content will improve.

Whether your passage is literary or non-literary, prose, verse or any other text type or genre, you will need to write about how the writer uses language, for what purpose, and for which audience; tone, imagery, rhythm, diction, mood, and other stylistic features characterise all language – we use them all the time, differently in different situations. The writer of your text made choices about all of these and more, choosing stylistic features to have the desired effect on the target audience. Imagery is not only found in verse; advertisers, story tellers, newsreaders, preachers, politicians, playwrights – anyone who uses language uses it for a purpose.

Always remember that when you analyse language, or comment on language use, you are not showing simply that you understand the content – this is not an exercise in comprehension – you must go further than summarising or paraphrasing the content. If your passage was written in the seventeenth century, you do not have to re-write it in modern English. Rather, you have to show that you understand what the purpose of the writer is, who she or he is writing for, and how the language works to achieve it. In this instance you would also think about context, since the period will have some impact on the sentencing and vocabulary.

In planning your analysis, you will need to address the following basic elements:

Content and form

At the simplest level, you need to show the examiner that you are aware of these two aspects of the passage. The *content* is the "story", the ideas, the feelings which the piece of writing conveys to you. The *form* is the structure, the shape, the genre in which the writer chooses to present the content. Is it an advertisement, an extract from a biography, a sonnet, a speech?

When you recognise the text type, you will look for the stylistic features most typical of it. For instance, if you are analysing a poem, you will automatically expect to find imagery – you will look for it. If you are analysing a speech, you will be looking for rhetorical devices. These features are called the *conventions* of the genre or text type. They are a good starting point for any analysis essay. It doesn't mean you won't be looking for everything else, but it does mean that you won't miss the obvious.

Form also includes visual texts – look at the section on advertising and the language of persuasion for more detailed guidance on this. Keep in mind that a picture is a text because it conveys meaning, so you will consider its use of imagery, its audience, purpose and context in the same way as you would a written text. In an exam, you are most likely to have to analyse visual texts which incorporate words – like advertisements, or campaign documents; nevertheless, you should practise "reading" visual texts just as you need to practise analysing written texts.

Tone and diction

Often the key to understanding a piece of writing comes not from the literal meaning of the words but from the *tone* (of voice) in which they are spoken, and you should try to read your extracts as expressively as possible. Imagine that you are reading them aloud. *"Let not the bat, nor the rat, nor the club-footed ghoul come near me"* (Prayer Before Birth, Louis MacNeice, analysed in chapter 5) will sound different from *"My love is like a red, red rose"* (A Red, Red Rose, Robert Burns), and that difference will help you to understand how the language works.

The kind of words the writer chooses is the *diction.* Someone who writes about *"an unusually high level of precipitation"* differs in purpose from someone who describes *"glittering diamond drops nestling in the grass".*

Rhythm

Rhythm is often more noticeable in verse than in prose; regular rhythm will give a steady and controlled effect to writing, whereas irregular rhythm will create a more disjointed, uncontrolled effect. In *Sacco Writes to his Son* Alun Lewis writes
"I hope this letter finds you in good health
My son, my comrade. Will you give my love
To Inez and your mother and my friends…"
using the lack of rhythm to highlight Dante's great sadness. However in *Prayer Before Birth* MacNeice uses rhythm to build up tension and make his message inescapable. A prose example of this is the opening of *The Hitchhiker's Guide to the Galaxy,* where a difference of rhythm changes the tempo and heralds the end of Earth. Rhythm performs many functions, and your analysis should address this.

Imagery

Imagery makes pictures with words. Though often people associate the use of imagery with literary writing, it is used in non-literary writing of all sorts as well – advertising is the obvious example. Choice of imagery helps to create the mood of a piece of writing, as well as enriching it. MacNeice creates a chilling view of the effects of society on the individual in *Prayer Before Birth* when he says
"… those who would freeze my
Humanity, would dragoon me into a lethal automaton…"
Equally, your extract may not use imagery – if it is an extract from a legal document, for instance, it will need to be factual, with no room for misinterpretation. Think of this in relation to the Universal Declaration of Human Rights, for instance – because it is universal it needs to be free of language that is rooted in a particular culture so that its meaning cannot be misunderstood. You can see this for yourself by looking it up in the appendix – the language is as simple as possible and absolutely clear.

Context

The effect a piece of writing has on the reader obviously varies with that person's experience – a European who is reading African literature for the first time will respond differently to *I Will Marry When I Want,* a Kenyan play by Ngugi, from a Kenyan reader or audience, who will be completely familiar with the dramatic conventions Ngugi uses. However, analysis should explain what effect the writer has on the reader, and how that effect is achieved. You will need to work out what effect the writer wants to achieve rather than starting with your own response; for instance if a passage is humorous but you do not find it funny, you will still identify and explain the use of comic devices. The key to this is to show how language has been used to create an effect, and why.

Another aspect of context is social, political or historical: if a writer is writing during a period of oppression, for instance, this will have an impact on how and why the text is written. Arthur Miller's *The Crucible* was written during the period of McCarthyism in 1950s USA – his criticism of the political rulers of the time had to be discrete, or he would have risked imprisonment; hence his choice of setting in seventeenth century Salem.

Purpose

This may not be immediately obvious, but of course it is fundamental; why write at all if you have nothing to communicate? The purpose may not be to achieve direct action, but it is always there and it informs the choices the writer makes. An advertisement wants you to buy the product advertised; a presidential candidate wants you to vote for her or him; a newspaper article wants to inform the reader about current events; a novel wants to reflect on some aspect of the human condition; a comedian wants to make you laugh – though in this case you also have ask *at what?* If your text comes from a work of fiction, don't satisfy yourself with saying that the purpose is to entertain – it will seldom be that simple!

Audience

Sometimes it will be obvious who the target audience is; often it won't be. You need to be thoughtful and specific in identifying it, though, and take into account the language that is used, including vocabulary as well as technical aspects of language use. You also need to consider the context in which the text is produced, how it is written, and what its purpose is. Put together, these will be clear enough, and you should be able to show by quoting examples from the text how they indicate audience. For example, instructions on how to make a longbow would have a very small audience of longbow enthusiasts – you know that from the nature of the activity. You would know from the nature of the narrative as well as from the language used if a story was intended for children. Sometimes you will know from the place you find the text who its target audience is, and one example of this is the documentary film about Joseph Kony. The documentary was made by a US charity raising awareness and money to stop the practice of forcing children to be soldiers. The target audience is global – it is everyone in the world; this is an unusually large target audience! Placing it on YouTube ensured that countless millions of people would have access to it.

With regard to advertising, your analysis should show that target audiences are specific, and are specifically targeted – when you see a picture of two adorable little children with the caption *"Don't be mean with the beans, Mum!"* you know that mothers are being targeted, and that the humour in the use of rhythm and rhyme is intended to engage them.

What these examples show is that the target audience is indicated in the text itself. You shouldn't have to wonder who it might be – you only need to read the text attentively and pick up the clues.

With literary texts, on the other hand, the question of audience is much less of an issue. It is not specific in the way it is with many other texts, and you may well not address it at all. Your analysis would not be helped if you said that the target audience is people who read literature – that is obvious. If the content makes it clear that there is a specific and more defined audience, identify and explain it; otherwise comment is pointless.

Use of language

How the writer uses grammatical structure is another aspect you will need to consider. It won't be something you comment on in all cases, because there may be nothing significant to say – only comment on what is there. But your text may be about accent and dialect, and if it is literary it may actually use accent or dialect. Or there you may need to comment on the paragraphing or sentence structure in a newspaper article – there is an enormous difference in the quality of writing between newspapers depending on the social and educational background of their reader base. Or a novelist may use a combination of short and long sentences to create suspense, as Douglas Adams does in the opening to *The Hitchhiker's Guide to the Galaxy*. Here he suggests an explosion that ends the world by using a series of short sentences.

Choice of vocabulary is also something you need to think about; is it sophisticated? Simple? If you say it is simple, you obviously need to explain what you mean by giving an example. Does it include slang? Or swearing? Is it technical? Does it include jargon? Are there lots of adjectives? Or none? If it is literary prose, does the author write in the present tense – if so, why, and with what effect?

You don't need to comment on these aspects of language use unless they appear in the text. Only comment on what is pertinent to your particular extract, and don't make a list of stylistic features that are not used unless you want to comment on their absence. But don't forget that you need to think about grammar and technical aspects of writing because it's all too easy to take them for granted and forget that here too language users make choices.

Content and form, tone and diction, rhythm, imagery, context, purpose, use of formal/grammatical aspects of language, audience – each of these elements in your analysis covers a range of stylistic devices which you must identify and explain in your analysis, relating them to the context in which the text was written, the purpose of the writer, and the audience for whom it was written.

The parts of the course and the assessment criteria

Part One: Language in Cultural Context

This part aims to develop your critical understanding and analytical skills. It does this by requiring you to study examples of specific text types in close detail.

Part One looks at *meaning* and how it changes in texts according to their specific context, purpose and audience. It also explores how language is fundamental to identity, both for the individual and for social groups – for example, this doesn't only mean whether it is English or French (for Canadians this would be an important reflection of who they are,) or Gikuyu or English (for many Kenyans this would be a very important aspect of their political context.) It also refers to the type of English you speak – for example, if you are British with family roots in the Caribbean, when, why and with whom do you choose to reflect your Caribbean roots in the language you use? You can see the importance of context here very clearly. The same considerations are true when you consider regional accents and dialects; why does the writer choose to use them in a text? And why, though you may well read literary texts making use of this device, are you unlikely to come across it in a newspaper? It is by focusing on texts reflecting such issues and ideas that Part One of the syllabus helps to develop your analytical skills.

This may sound difficult, but as you read more and more texts, you will realise that these ideas crop up all the time in daily life. For example, think about the language choices you make every day – you might well use colloquial language or even slang with your friends, but you would choose a much more formal register if you were talking to your head teacher or a visitor. Part One of the course is about recognising that *meaning* is created by the choices we make whenever we use language, taking into account who we're talking to or writing for, and why.

Aspects of your study of language use may have drawn attention to accent and dialect; the dominance of global languages; the increasing disappearance of minority languages; social status; gender and sexuality; translation; multilingualism – the list of possibilities is long, and you will have read texts about many of them.

The aim is to help you to:

- Analyse how audiences and purpose affect the structure and content of texts.

- Analyse the impact of the ways in which language changes.

- Demonstrate an awareness of how language and meaning are shaped by culture and context.

These are called **learning outcomes** and they sum up what the course hopes you will be able to achieve in your final assessments. You will see that they are reflected directly in criteria A and B.

Part Two: Language and mass communication

Part Two also requires you to look at specific texts in detail, in order to develop your critical awareness and analytical skills.

While Part One focuses on what influences the way we use and understand language, Part Two focuses on the means through which communication occurs globally and impacts on our lives constantly: the mass media. The two parts are closely interconnected, and it is likely that you will have looked at many texts from both perspectives. This part of the syllabus is not testing your knowledge of the media as a phenomenon; rather, by requiring you to look at specific examples of texts from different media, it is developing your awareness of the way the media text types influence how language is used, and how that influences what we understand.

For example, in Part One you may have looked at the language of prejudice and the nature of stereotypes, while in Part Two you would analyse an advertisement using stereotypes or reflecting widely held prejudices to sell its product. Or, you may have studied and analysed a campaign promoting equality, which would have challenged stereotypes.

All of this is encapsulated in the Part Two aims, which are to help you to do the following:

- To examine different forms of communication within the media – that is, make the link between the form and the ways it is used with the language it uses, so you can be analytical in your examination.

- To show an awareness of the potential for education, political or ideological influence of the media – that is, by looking at, for example, specific political speeches or perhaps a campaign about consumerism and climate change. Such influence can be for good or bad purposes, and the same stylistic features serve both; you are expected to analyse the way language is used for its purpose rather than judging the purpose – critical analysis is not subjective.

- To show the way mass media use language and image to inform, persuade or entertain. This includes identifying the stylistic features the text uses, its visual presentation or layout, its use of persuasive devices, its target audience and its style and register.

Here again, if you check the assessment criteria, you will find that these learning outcomes are reflected in criteria A and B.

Part Three: Literature: texts and contexts

Keep in mind that while Part Three texts are assessed specifically in Paper Two, this section requires close study of literary texts and their contexts, and so this will expand your experience of the uses of language to communicate. The literary texts you read, just like the non-literary and media texts, are written for a purpose, within a context, and for an audience; they use the same range of stylistic features, maybe using some more than others; they make choices of style, register, vocabulary, grammar, accent and dialect. So even if you are not going to be tested on your Part Three texts in Paper

One, the critical reading involved is absolutely relevant and useful for the development of the skills you need for Paper One. What you learn here you can apply elsewhere.

In Paper One you may well be required to analyse a literary extract – it could be a poem, prose or play extract, or an extract from any other literary genre. Just as Parts One and Two focus on non-literary text types to develop your understanding of how language is used, Parts Three and Four focus on literary texts, and are equally important for Paper One.

The desired learning outcomes for Part Three, as we have seen, are primarily directed at Paper Two, but they also target the Paper One assessment criteria A and B. You should be able to:

- Consider the changing historical, cultural and social contexts in which particular texts are written and received.

- Demonstrate how the formal elements of the text, genre and structure can not only be seen to influence meaning but can also be influenced by context.

- Understand the attitudes and values expressed by literary texts and their impact on readers.

Part Four: Literature: critical study

The Individual Oral Commentary (IOC) assesses the texts you study for Part Four by means of close analysis of a short extract from one of them. Paper One contains unseen texts, and is written; but it asks for the same critical awareness and the same analytical skills as the oral commentary.

For Part Four you learn to do the following by studying your two texts (if you are following the course at standard level) or three (at higher level):

- How to read a literary text critically and in detail, understanding elements like characterisation and narrative development and theme.

- How to identify and analyse the ideas and thematic preoccupations of a literary text.

- To recognise, understand and use appropriate critical vocabulary (refer to the list of terms at the end of the guide to see these).

This means that every part of the course is designed to develop or enhance the critical and analytical skills you will need for Paper One.

Is there a standard structure for an analysis essay?

Paper One at standard level is different from the higher paper; at standard level there are two extracts, each a different text type, and candidates have to choose one to analyse; they include in their analysis comment on the importance of context, audience, purpose and formal and stylistic features. At higher level there are two pairs of extracts, and candidates have to choose one pair to analyse comparatively.

It is worth keeping in mind that visual images will not be reproduced in colour for the purposes of the exam.

So far we have looked at what is entailed in the analysis of a single text, because even if you are going to comment on two texts comparatively, your starting point will be with the detailed analysis of each one individually. The section that follows this one says more about higher level and the comparative analysis.

There is no one optimum structure. Different texts will evoke different responses, and you will want to start your analysis in different places. However, the questions in the section about the language of persuasion form a good basis structure; if you work through them carefully, referring specifically to the text, you will have a solidly structured analysis essay for many media text types.

Similarly, if you were to go through the points in the section on the analysis of literary texts, you would have a comprehensive commentary. The points all need to be addressed, and there is no harm at all in having a mental checklist of features you need to consider, so long as you only write about the pertinent items on it. The checklist must not become a rigid formula.

The starting point

Most extracts will have something about the content or the way they are written that stands out for you at first reading; if it is satirical, your analysis will explain what is being satirised and how the satire is achieved. To do that you will have to go through all the elements we have already listed. You would, in the case of a satirical text, probably want to start with the object of the satire and the reason for it. If your extract were humorous, you would probably want to start with the humour in a similar way. The best place for you to start is with your initial response to the extract, the feelings or ideas it evokes. If it makes you laugh, feel sad or angry; or if you find it informative or original; if what strikes you first is that it is very descriptive, or is written in short sentences, or is strongly rhetorical; if there is something very particular about the narrative voice – whatever your response, it will be a good place to start your analysis.

You do need to plan your essay; careful preparation will enable you to write more coherently and make it less likely that you will need to add extra paragraphs or sentences at the end, squeezed into margins or tacked on out of sequence – this sort of thing can seriously affect your marks for criterion C, which addresses organisation and development.

The example below shows how you might approach a media text in preparation for your essay, with a student's annotations.

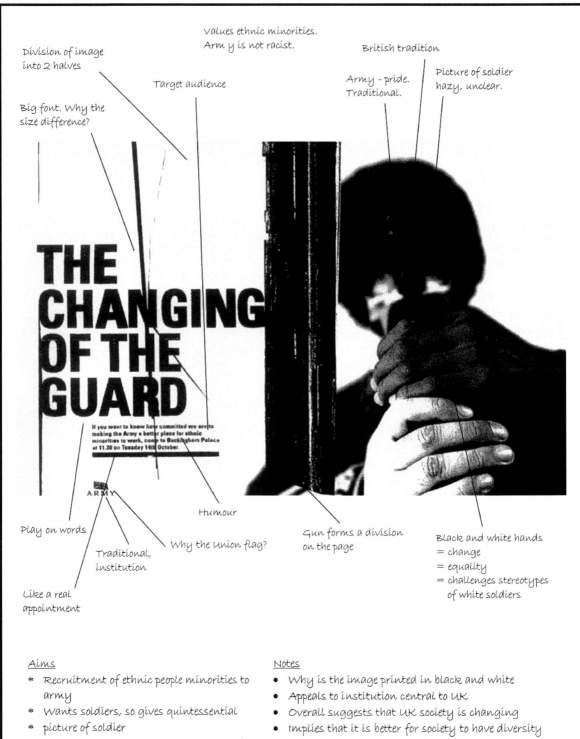

Values ethnic minorities. Arm y is not racist.

Division of image into 2 halves

Target audience

British tradition

Army – pride. Traditional.

Picture of soldier hazy, unclear.

Big font. Why the size difference?

THE CHANGING OF THE GUARD

If you want to know how committed we are to making the Army a better place for ethnic minorities to work, come to Buckingham Palace at 11.30 on Tuesday 14th October.

ARMY

Play on words

Humour

Gun forms a division on the page

**Black and white hands
= change
= equality
= challenges stereotypes
of white soldiers**

Traditional, institution

Why the Union flag?

Like a real appointment

<u>Aims</u>

* Recruitment of ethnic people minorities to army
* Wants soldiers, so gives quintessential
* picture of soldier
* Means/message—the army has changed/ is changing... 'Changing' in headline
* And image—black sharing with white

<u>Notes</u>

• Why is the image printed in black and white
• Appeals to institution central to UK
• Overall suggests that UK society is changing
• Implies that it is better for society to have diversity
• 1994—1998 was a period of rapidly growing awareness of the need to challenge racism. This is reflected in the advert
• Army had been seen to be racist in both high profile news and in popular films
• Audience is assumed to be anti-racist, sharing the "better place" idea—that is the idea we identify with
• If this appeared in the years between 1994—1998, it would have been part of a bigger campaign.

Planning notes

- It is fine to write down, as questions, the things you don't understand – they will usually become clear as you continue; you will make links.

- When you have made as many annotations as you can, go through the list on pages 19 – 21 and check that you have thought about all the different sections.

- Use the questions to go back over the poster, so you can look for things you may have missed first time.

- Now you are ready to plan your essay. Group your annotations according to the point you want them to illustrate – presentation, or target audience, or language, or values, or any of the other categories. These will be your paragraphs, and need to show a development in your analysis. This poster fits the order on pages 19 – 21.

- Think about the introduction. Keep it brief and focused. You don't need to write a history of the British army by way of introduction, and you don't need to make any general comments about the need to have an army. There is not a formula for the introduction, but you need to show in it that you know what the main purpose of the text is, and maybe its most noticeable features.

The introduction

A possible introduction for this poster could be:

"This text is a recruitment poster for the British Army, and its target audience is made clear by its emphasis on change, while it reinforces the traditional qualities people associate with the institution. This is emphasised by the connection between the illustration and the words."

These introductory sentences show that you have grasped the most significant aspects of the poster; and they indicate the direction your analysis will take. You have not started the analysis, which will be the main body of your essay; and you have stayed completely focused on the text, with no unnecessary digressions. It is not the only possible introduction – it is an example of the appropriate approach.

You should avoid the conversational approach. This sentence, for instance, may well be true in a general sense: "Every army needs to ensure that it has enough soldiers; in peace and war, countries need to have a well trained army to maintain the safety of their people." It is not relevant to this poster, does not refer to ideas reflected in it, and gives no indication that you have got to grips with the content of the text you are being assessed on. It is not a good introduction.

The conclusion also needs to be brief and focused. Pick up the main points from your analysis. Looking back at the annotations, a conclusion to this analysis might read like this:

"This army recruitment poster targets the minority ethnic population. It acknowledges that in the past the army has not been diverse, and suggests that it has been racist. Using a variety of stylistic features, it appeals to its target audience, possible recruits from minority

ethnic groups, by assuring them that the army is changing, and that they can be part of this radical change."

In this way, you sum up the purpose, identify the target audience, and link these to the text itself.

Planning notes for the higher level essay

The instruction for Paper One at higher level will ask candidates to choose either Section A or Section B; each will consist of two extracts representing different text types; they could be literary or non-literary. Candidates will be asked to analyse, compare and contrast the two texts on the section they choose, commenting, on the similarities and differences between them. Just as at standard level, there will be the instruction to include comment on context, purpose, and formal and stylistic features.

When you have chosen the pair of extracts you prefer, your starting point is to annotate them both in the way suggested above. Identify the theme or idea they have in common – it could be anything. You could have a newspaper article about a war and the transcript of an interview with a government minister justifying participation in it; you could have an advertisement for spring bulbs and a poem about daffodils. You will show that because the meaning they want to communicate is different, because they have different purposes, different audiences, different contexts, the authors use language differently. You will explore and explain these differences, and similarly describe any similarities you identify.

Try comparing the following song lyrics with the army recruitment poster on page 29; these two texts could well be chosen to go together for a section of a higher level Paper One.

For higher level Paper One you start planning your essay by annotating both texts, as this student has. The last section lists the similarities and differences between the two texts.

The Universal Soldier

War is universal

He's 5 foot 2 and he's 6 feet 4
He fights with missiles and with spears
He's all of 31 and he's only 17.
He's been a soldier for a thousand years

- Could be anyone
- From any time
- Old or young

An idea, not a real person
Symbolic

All religions tell you not to fight

He's a catholic, a Hindu, an atheist, a Jain
A Buddhist, and a Baptist and Jew.
And he knows he shouldn't kill
And he knows he always will kill
You'll for me my friend and me for you

Of any religion

Human nature

Nationalism is dangerous

And He's fighting for Canada.
He's fighting for France.
He's fighting for the USA.
And he's fighting for the Russians.
And he's fighting for Japan
And he thinks we'll put an end to war this way.

Nationalism

War is illogical

And He's fighting for democracy,
He's fighting for the reds
He says it's for the peace of all.
He's the one, who must decide,
who's to live and who's to die.
And he never sees the writing on the wall.

Contradiction — TOK
So not politicians or generals, just ordinary person
Widely known aphorism

War dehumanises

But without him,
how would Hitler have condemned him at Dachau?
Without him Caesar would have stood alone
He's the one who gives his body
as a weapon of the war.
And without him all this killing can't go on

To shock, make it serious and real
simile

Can't blame other people

He's the universal soldier
And he really is the blame
His orders comes from
far away no more.

Worldwide — there are wars everywhere
That is, it is not someone else's fault

It is our fault

They come from here and there.
And you and me.
And brothers can't you see.
This is not the way we put an end to war

2nd person; audience engaged in conversation

Purpose of poem is to persuade audience against war

Song lyrics by Buffy Sainte-Marie, 1963

33

Rhythm

- It's a song; so rhythm is very regular. It changes in the last verse to become slower – gives more impact to strong message
- Conversational tone
  Each verse addresses a different bad aspect of war

Similarities

- Both address their target audience. IE use 2nd person of the verb
- Conversational tone
- About soldiers
- Use aphorisms everyone knows to convey their meaning ("changing of the guard", writing on the wall")

Differences

- Creative nature of song lyrics = rhythm, more imagery
- Spiritual appeal of lyrics
- Patriotic appeal of poster text
- Visual images underline meaning in poster
- Changes of rhythm underline meaning in the song
- View of soldiers - Unquestionably good in poster; absolutely bad in lyrics. In fact, in poster, war is not mentioned – the army is seen as a benefit to society. Lyrics see soldier as a destroyer of society

Target audience – Potential recruits/voting public

Purpose – to recruit/to get people to vote against war

Introduction

A possible introduction could be as follows:

The subject in both text 1 and text 2 is soldiers. The recruitment poster for the Army uses visual images to add to the patriotic message that being a soldier is a good occupation, whereas the use of rhythmical poetic devices in the song underlines the message that being a soldier is bad for society; this shows that while the texts share a subject, their purposes are very different.

Main body/development

You could start the main body of the essay by commenting fully on text 1, possibly saying:

Text 1 is an army recruitment poster, so its purpose is to persuade people to join the army. It therefore uses a variety of persuasive devices to make the life of a soldier look desirable. It is particularly targeting people from minority ethnic groups, and the main focus of the poster is on the change that this represents. This is evident in the large lettering caption," The changing of the guard"

- Look at the way people are presented – the photograph is rather blurry, so you can't see if the person in it is from a minority ethnic group. Go through the questions on the presentation of people, discussing any that are relevant. You could include comment on the way the song represents soldiers here, for instance saying that Buffy Sainte Marie describes a soldier as "a weapon of the war" and says he has been so throughout history. This will give you a coherent paragraph, and will include an element of comparison.

- It will link conveniently with the second paragraph, on presentation/format; it is a poster, and its aim is persuasive, so it is like an advertisement. The questions in the list continue to be relevant. There will be little here to say about the song, so don't force a comparison.

- The next paragraph in your essay could discuss the use of text and language. You will explain the meaning of the pun that dominates the poster – the changing of the guard – and implications it has about the racist nature of the Army in the past and its intention to change for the better now: "A better place for ethnic minorities." Show how the language appeals to convention and tradition, and link this to the images. Identify the use of suggestion, and the avoidance of direct tackling of the issue the poster is really tackling – the racism that has prevented people from ethnic minorities from joining the Army. There are far fewer words in the poster than in the song, and in the poster the images work with the words to convey part of the meaning.

- Group your annotations suitably to address the question on the poster overall and anything you think relevant about its wider context.

- Use a comparative linking phrase like "*unlike the poster, the song has a global rather than a national audience. Its subject is also universal, not just for one nation, culture or religion.*" Now write about the annotations you made to start with, and analyse the song. When you can, refer to the poster; so, when you write about language use, for instance, you will refer to what you have already said briefly about content and form, identifying the difference of purpose implied by the difference of form/text type between the two texts.

- Tone and diction will also give you a chance to refer back to the poster. You could write about language use in this section of your essay.

- You have already mentioned the use of rhythm in the song without writing in detail, so come back to it now and expand your comments.

- In the song, the soldier is symbolic, representative of humanity's darker side, the side that doesn't think either clearly or independently. Comment on the sustained image of the hypocritical soldier.

- The examination paper will always give you the date of publication, or writing if that is more appropriate, of the exam texts. Unless that information helps your analysis, don't refer to it; but it could be significant when you think about context. In the case of the song, you might have noticed that it was written at the height of the period of anti-war fervour, with fear of the potential of nuclear catastrophe very much a feature of the cold war years. This would undoubtedly have been part of the reason why the song writer created these lyrics, and people who felt as she did – many, especially young people – would have been her target audience.

- You will have mentioned purpose and audience already when you wrote about the poster, but now you can write about these aspects of both texts. It will bring you to the end still thinking about the similarities and differences between them,

Conclusion

Again, the conclusion needs to be short. You have to show that you have contrasted the two extracts, looked at the similarities and differences between the ways they use all aspects of language, and recognised the implications for language used of purpose and audience in both. A possible conclusion could be:

These two texts have very different purposes; the poster aims to recruit soldiers, while the song aims to stop people from being soldiers or thinking there is anything good about being a soldier. The poster is a medium that will be most effective in reaching the Army's target audience, while the song, written in the context of anti-war protest songs, is most appropriate for the singer's audience; both arise very directly from their context.

Have a go!

Look back at these two texts and the way this student has annotated them. Make your own annotations, add to the ones already there. Think about your own response – after all, this will be your starting point. You are not going to say "I like text 1 because…" or "I do not agree with the point of view of the song writer…" because this is not a personal essay; it is a formal critical analysis, with its formal, objective conventions. Nevertheless, how you feel about a text will influence the way you think about its meaning and how you plan your essay.

If you are taking the course at standard level, try both texts separately – it is good practice for you to try out lots of different text types. If you are taking the course at higher level, have a go at planning your own comparative analysis of the two texts. The student annotations and these notes will guide you through the process.

The next section will give you more practice; it includes a complete sample Paper One at higher level, with an essay script responding to it, followed by examiner comments and marks awarded. Reading all of these will help you to understand what is required of you in the exam.

Standard level candidates could practise on all four extracts, while higher level candidates could practise on both pairs.

Sample paper one: higher level

Choose either Section A or Section B

Section A

Analyse, compare and contrast the following two texts. Include comments on the similarities and differences between the two texts and the significance of context, purpose, and formal and stylistic features.

Text 1

RABBIT IN MIXER SURVIVES

A baby rabbit fell into a quarry's mixing machine yesterday and came out in the middle of a concrete block. But the rabbit still had the strength to dig its way free before the block set.

The tiny creature was scooped up with 30 tons of sand, then swirled and pounded through the complete mixing process. Mr Michael Hooper, the machine operator, found the rabbit shivering on top of the solid concrete block, its coat still with fragments. A hole from the middle of the block and paw marks showed the escape route.

Mr Reginald Denslow, manager of J. R. Pratt and Sons' quarry at Kilmingotn, near Axminster, Devon, said: 'This rabbit must have a lot more than nine lives to go through this machine. I just don't know how it avoided being suffocated, ground, squashed or cut in half.' With the 30 tons of sand, it was dropped into a weighing hopper and carried by conveyor to an overhead mixer where it was whirled around with gallons of water.

From there the rabbit was swept to a machine which hammers wet concrete into blocks by pressure of 100 lb per square inch. The rabbit was encased in a block eighteen inches long, nine inches high and six inches thick. Finally the blocks were ejected onto the floor to dry and the dazed rabbit clawed itself free. 'We cleaned him up, dried him by the electric fire, then he hopped away,' Mr Denslow said.

Daily Telegraph

Text 2

"Tell us a story Grandad"
The bunny rabbits implored
"About the block of concrete
Out of which you clawed."

"Tell every gory detail
Of how you struggled free
From the teeth of the iron monster
Ans swam through a quicksand sea."

"How you battled with the Humans
(And the part we like the most)
Your escape from the raging fire
When they held you there to roast."

The old adventurer smiled
And waved a wrinkled paw
"All right children, settle down,
I'll tell it just once more."

His thin nose started twitching
Near-blind eyes began to flood
As the part that doesn't age
Drifted back to bunnyhood.

When spring was king of the seasons
And days were built to last
When thunder was merely thunder
Not a distant quarry last.

How, leaving the warren one morning
Looking for somewhere to play,
He'd wandered into the woods
And there had lost his way.

When suddenly without warning
The earth gave way, and he fell
Off the very edge of the world
Into the darkness of Hell.

Sharp as the colour of a carrot
On a new-born bunny's tongue
Was the picture he recalled
Of that day when he was young.

Trance-formed now by the memory
His voice was close to tears
But the story he was telling
Was falling on deaf ears.

There was giggling and nudging
And lots of "sssh - he'll hear"
For it was a trick, a game they played
Grown crueler with each year.

"Poor old Grandad" they tittered
As they one by one withdrew
"He's told it all so often
He now believes it's true."

Young rabbits need fresh carrots
And his had long grown stale
So they left the old campaigner
Imprisoned in his tale.

Petrified by memories
Haunting ever strong
Encased in a block of time
Eighteen inches long.

* * *

Alone in a field in Devon
An old rabbit is sitting, talking,
When out of the wood, at the edge of
the world
A man with a gun comes walking.

Roger McGough

39

Section B

Analyse, compare and contrast the following two texts. Include comments on the similarities and differences between the two texts and the significance of context, purpose, and formal and stylistic features.

Text 3

The mainstream media were transfixed last week by a meme – an infectious idea. Hard-bitten news editors – the professionals who pride themselves on knowing what will happen before it happens – were discomfited to discover that their teenage kids knew something they didn't know. That something was a YouTube video that had been spreading at an astonishing rate. Entitled Kony 2012, it is a 30-minute film made by a campaigning organisation called Invisible Children.

Its goal was to raise awareness of the activities of Joseph Kony, a Ugandan warlord who leads the Lord's Resistance Army, in the hope of bringing him to justice. Kony and his LRA are distinguished by their violence and brutality, their weird ideology and – crucially for the purposes of the video – their practice of abducting children and turning them into child soldiers. This last practice has led to the bizarre
phenomenon of "night commuting", in which Ugandan children leave their villages at night in order to sleep in towns, where they are supposedly less vulnerable to kidnapping by Kony and his goons.

Invisible Children is a US-based campaigning group, founded in 2004 by film-makers, which has been working in Uganda – building radio networks, monitoring LRA movements and helping displaced children and families.

It has focused on raising awareness of the LRA and on influencing US government policy towards the region. It is believed that its campaigning was at least partly
responsible for Barack Obama's decision in 2010 to send 100 military advisers to the Ugandan military to assist in capturing Kony.

The YouTube video is a brilliant piece of film-making, in two ways. First, it has a compelling, simple narrative: Kony is a really bad guy and his capture will end
suffering for the people of northern Uganda. If US viewers do their bit by influencing their politicians, the world's superpower will take action and Kony will be
captured.

Second, it conveys this message in a seductive way, with film-maker Jason Williams explaining to his five-year-old son that this Kony is a monster and that dad's job is capturing him. What's not to like?

Jason's message was released last Monday. By Thursday it had amassed 26 million views. When I last looked at it on Saturday it was up to 63 million views (with 1,212,109 "likes" and only 59,702 "dislikes"). So, in the jargon of the day, it's "gone viral". In that sense, it represents the most successful manipulation of our new media ecosystem to date because "virality" is what every huckster, politician and advertiser now craves – but very few achieve.

John Naughton, Observer (March 2012)

Text 4

First we ran around the building for a few minutes, and then we began to learn how to crawl in the bushes nearby. Corporal Gadafi would hold his fist up, and when he brought it down, we fell into the bushes and crawled quickly, without producing much sound, until we reached a designated tree. Then we immediately got up and crouched to take cover behind other trees. Afterward, we would run back to the training ground. The corporal didn't say much during the initial stage of training. All he said was "Not bad, "Terrible", and "Faster." He mostly used hand gestures, which he said was the only thing that would be used once we were out there. He would point to the clearing, where "words could cost you a bullet in the head." He would then smile drily and widen his eyes for us to laugh with him. After we had done the running, crawling, and crouching many times, we were allowed to have some bread and custard. The corporal gave us one minute to get the food and eat it. Whatever we hadn't eaten was taken away at the end of sixty seconds. None of us was able to finish eating on the first day, but within a week we could eat any food in a minute. It was the only part of the training that we mastered.

After the late breakfast, we lined up facing the corporal, who handed us AK-47s. When it was my turn, he looked at me intensely, as if he was trying to tell me that he was giving me something worth cherishing. He poked my chest with his finger and walked around me. When he came back to the front, he stared at me some more, his red eyes and dark face twitching. He bared his teeth as if he were preparing to attack, and my legs began to shake, when he started to smile. Before I could smile with him, he had stopped, and the veins on his forehead stood up. Still looking straight at me, he reached into a wooden crate and pulled out the gun. He took out the magazine and handed me the AK with two hands. I hesitated for a bit, but he pushed the gun against my chest. With trembling hands I took the gun, saluted him, and ran to the back of the line, still holding the gun but afraid to look at it. I had never held a gun that long before and it frightened me. The closest thing to it had been a toy gun made out of bamboo when I was seven. My playmates and I carved them and played war games in the coffee farms and unfinished buildings at my grandmother's village. *Paw paw*, we would go, and whoever did it first would announce to the rest whom he had killed.

From *A Long Way Gone,* Ishmael Beah (2008)

Sample Paper One Script – higher level

The two different texts by Ishmael Beah and John Naughton both have the common theme of child soldiers, but from the different ways they use language it becomes clear that their purpose and audience are not the same.

The article written by John Norton and published in a newspaper called The Observer analyses the video that is the main part of the Kony 2012 campaign against the use of child soldiers by the Uganda Lords Resistance Army. It is written in a factual and objective way. It is divided into seven paragraphs, each one describing a different aspect of the topic. In the first paragraph, 'Kony 2012' and its background are introduced. While the article aims to be objective overall, the author uses emotive vocabulary in paragraph two to engage the reader, in highlighting the reasons why the campaigning organisation 'Invisible Children' undertook to start the 'Kony 2012' campaign. In order to achieve this effect the vocabulary used includes words such as 'violence', 'brutality', 'weird ideology' and 'bizarre phenomenon', which have negative connotations and will cause the reader to react in a certain way.

In paragraphs three to four however, the author uses factual information ("Invisible Children is a US based campaigning group"; "Obama's decision in 2012 to send 100 military advisers to the Ugandan military") to remain neutral and to inform the reader about objective facts.

Following the factual information, the author analyses the 'Kony 2012' video itself critically; while the text states that "the YouTube video is a brilliant piece of film making", it also points out its strong simplicity ("Kony is a really bad guy and his capture will end suffering for the people of Northern Uganda"). This is also done deliberately to make the reader understand both the positive and the negative aspects of the campaigning video in order to be able to critically evaluate it.

The author's criticism of the 'Kony 2012' campaign becomes clear in the last paragraph, in which 'virality' is described as "the most successful manipulation of our new media system" and as "what every huckster politician and advertiser now craves".

Generally, the article uses complex sentences and a broad vocabulary, which suggests an educated target audience. This is clear in the author's criticism of 'Kony 2012, in which he assumes that the reader has the same knowledge about the ways narratives are used for examples, to have a specific effect on the reader. The Observer is also commonly thought of as a sophisticated newspaper rather than a tabloid, which further suggests that the target audience is educated people with some form of academic background.

The purpose of this article is mainly to inform the reader about what 'Kony 2012' is and how its success can be explained, but it also aims to make the reader think critically about the phenomenon of virality and to encourage critical evaluation of the 'Kony 2012' campaign and the way it uses language.

The autobiographical text 'A Long Way Gone' by Ishmael Beah, published in 2008, also has the theme of child soldiers, but its purpose and use of language are different from the newspaper article's. In this extract, the author describes his own experience of what appears to be a training camp for child soldiers.

The text can be divided into two parts. The first paragraph describes events that took place over a certain period of time, picking some examples to create a more vivid picture of what happened; the second paragraph talks about one particular event in detail. By using structures such as "He would point to", "He would smile drily" and "Corporal Gadafi would hold his fist up" the author creates a more general overview of his time at the camp. Both paragraphs make use of emotive language and the text is written in the first person, using the author's narrative voice, to give the reader an understanding of the author's internal emotional experience and to create an emotional response in the reader.

Generally the author uses relatively short sentences so that the reader will be able to read and understand the text quickly. This creates a sense of immediacy. The reader can feel the tense and fearful atmosphere of Beah's life in the camp and the way he was coerced into accepting the gun without the opportunity to think about it. In order to further highlight the tense atmosphere and the painful emotions associated with it, the author uses direct quotes that show the brutality of the adult soldiers; "words could cost you a bullet in the head" for example.

Beah further creates empathy and a sense of immediacy with his detailed description of people: "his red eyes and dark face" and "and the veins on his forehead stood up." These quotations also make the reader feel that the frightening soldier is very near which adds to the sense of terror.

In the last five lines the author, in a flashback, describes a childhood memory. He uses cheerful and happy vocabulary like "toy", "grandmother's village", "pawpaw" and "my playmates" which create a sense of the innocence and safety of childhood as it ought to be. This contrasts sharply with the horror of Beah's experiences at the training camp. This evokes feelings of great sadness in the reader for the horrific life of Beah and the other child soldiers.

The target audience is broader than for the Observer article, since the book will appeal not only to people interested in human rights issues but also to a wider reading literate public. The purpose of this text is also very different from that of the Observer article as its main aim is to raise awareness about these terrible events by creating an emotional response so that the reader will sympathise with the child soldiers. Though the two texts differ in their target audience, purpose and their choice of language, there are also similarities. Both texts aim to raise awareness about the plight of child soldiers and while Beah's autobiography does appeal to his audience emotionally, the criticism in John Naughton's article of the over-emotive nature of the video does not apply to Beah's writing. So both texts use emotive language, both are objective and both use factual information.

The chief difference between them is contextual: one is reviewing a primary text while the other actually is a primary text. The very direct language of Ishmael Beah's autobiography makes his writing authentic and its simplicity contrasts with the sophistication of John Naughton's critical position. This means that the reader understands more about the plight of child soldiers from the second text because that is its primary purpose while one can only infer information from the first text. It is clear therefore that while these two texts have the same topic as their subject, their different contexts, audiences and purposes make them very different from each other.

Sample examiner comment

Criterion A – Understanding and comparison of the texts

The essay shows good understanding of the similarities and differences between the texts, and recognises that different text types imply different audiences; it shows understanding of the connection between language choices and audience, and illustrates effectively with quotations from the texts.

Understanding of the purpose of text 4 is good; the essay identifies not only the broad aim to raise awareness but also to create sympathy with a group that usually invites fear. The purpose of text 3 is less clearly explained, but the essay does show, with supporting textual evidence, that the aim is to comment on the new media phenomenon rather than the issue. The essay also reflects the critical nature of the text as a review of the documentary. Good understanding of the implications of context is demonstrated throughout.

Criterion B – Understanding of the use and effects of stylistic features

The effects of stylistic features are recognised and illustrated with examples from the texts, as when the lexical set (of violence) is referenced in the first extract. The effect of emotive writing and use of imagery is described effectively. Clear understanding of the effects of stylistic features is evident and linked to the way the texts create and convey meaning to their readers; technical aspects of writing are also taken into account in considering text, audience and purpose.

Criterion C – Organisation and development

The comparative analysis is well organised, with a clear sense of development. Each text is analysed in detail, and comparisons are made within that framework; equal attention is paid to both texts. The introduction would have been improved if it had briefly identified the main difference in purpose between the two texts, but the essay does pick that reference up later. The conclusion takes the introduction into account.

Criterion D – Language

The language is clear, varied and accurate. The register is consistently appropriate, the vocabulary and sentence structure sophisticated, with no contrived formality. The essay is cogent.

Overall comment

This is a sound response to Paper One; it demonstrates understanding of the idea prompting both texts and accurately identifies the differences of topic, approach, audience, purpose and context. It is clearly organised, and coherently written, and it refers in detail to the extracts to evidence its analytical points. It avoids generalisations and exaggerated formality of style, and explains how stylistic features work rather than just identifying them.

Analysing an exam text – final preparation

Points to think about before you start

The aim of analysing a text is to explain how language is used to convey meaning. Expressed like this, it seems straightforward, but often being good at text analysis, orally or in writing, is seen as a gift some people have and others don't.

This is not the case: it is a skill you can learn rather than a gift you are born with; systematic practice will help you to acquire it.

There are a few basic points to keep in mind, and taking these on board will keep you properly focused, however you decide to structure your essay.

The first two of these are imperative, and, (to show how important it is,) are really different ways of saying the same thing:

- Do not be general. Always refer to the text to substantiate the points you make.
- Make specific points and illustrate them with quotations.
- Remember that this is analysis, not comprehension – do not summarise the text.
- While you read the text, think about its context, purpose and audience.
- As you read a text in preparation for analysis, underline or highlight anything you think needs comment – it doesn't matter at this stage if you don't know what the comment should be; you will find by the end that the complete picture of your annotations will help you to start your analysis.
- Ask yourself broad questions to help yourself into the analysis:
    - What is the message?
    - What is the mood or atmosphere?
    - Does anything stand out about the grammar, sentence structure and length, lexical fields and technical vocabulary
    - What is the register? Is it formal/ informal? Public? Personal?
    - Is it funny? Sad? Happy? Serious?
    - Is it emotive? Objective?
    - Does it use imagery? Or not use it? This will, in many cases, relate to the text type.
- What text type is it? What characteristics of this type of text might you be likely to find and therefore be looking for?
- Is there anything that strikes you about the time or place it was written, or the person who wrote it, that helps the reader (you) to understand it?

You will find more questions to ask as you continue to read – the more you ask, the better, because your answers to them will form the basis of your analysis essay. Note the answers on the text itself, and identify the actual words in the text that make you answer the questions the way you do. Think about the technical critical vocabulary you have learned during the course – there is a list of these in the Glossary at the end, and it will be useful as a checklist and reminder. You will finish with a heavily annotated text, and all you'll have to do is decide how to organise this information coherently so that your essay is effectively structured.

Chapter Three

External assessment – Paper two

Paper Two assesses your response to the literary works you study in Part Three of the course: **Texts and Contexts.** These two elements are so closely connected that it is almost impossible to talk about one without the other. They are addressed separately here only for convenience, so that you understand their significance and take them both into account when you plan your exam essay. Much of what follows applies more conveniently to prose works – novels, short stories, plays, literary non-fiction – than to poetry. Poetry will be discussed in detail in the section on Internal Assessment.

Part Three focuses on literary works, but on this course, works of literature are not seen as entities that stand alone, independent of their context or their reader; they are seen as a way of conveying meaning and responding to the human condition like any other means of expression. They are no more or less important than any other text type as a way of reflecting our experiences as human beings. The study of literature is traditionally a discipline of its own with its own specific conventions, and Part Three expects you to be entirely familiar with these. In addition, your critical appreciation of a work must include considerations of context, and how integral it is to that work.

The following section explains the nature of Part Three of the course and suggests ways of applying it to the exam.

Contexts

What is context?

As the title of Part Three suggests, the course is based on what can be described as an inclusive understanding of the nature of literature. It suggests that context matters as much as the text itself, and in a way this course sees literary analysis through a slightly different lens; on other courses, while you would always be expected to know about the background of a literary work, it would not be seen as being of critical importance in the analysis. Only the text itself, in such a way of seeing literary criticism, is the subject of the analysis.

In the Language A: Language and Literature course there is an acknowledgement of the fact that no literary work is separate from the circumstances that surround it; part of its meaning depends on the situation it arises from – its context. It is not simply that the reader needs to be aware of the background in order to understand the text but that the context of a literary work is intrinsic to it – that means it would not have come into existence without the particular set of circumstances in which it was written. These are part of its meaning.

The ideas or concerns that most people share in a period or place are reflected not only in the choice of narrative and the themes explored, but also in the ways characters are portrayed, the language used, the imagery, the stylistic features used, and also in what is omitted: works don't have to address a situation or idea directly. They may simply assume that there is a way of behaving that is right, (or wrong,) because in their society it is so, and so they don't have to address the moral view at all. You can see this if you think about the way attitudes to the role of women in society are reflected in different works: a novel written in a period when women were completely subordinate to men would write within that understanding – at the time it was written, people would not think "That's not fair." A hundred years later, readers would identify that as a thematic issue and they certainly would think it unfair.

Another way of showing how important context is for analysis and critical understanding is to think about how some works can be understood in a completely different way at different times. This won't be equally true of all texts but, to illustrate the point, there are many texts written during the European colonial era that, when they were written seemed favourable in their treatment of colonised countries and peoples. With the understanding history has given us of the true nature of colonialism, we can now see that even a genuinely well meaning work can be patronising, and may be perpetuating negative stereotypes. If you have studied *Othello* or The *Merchant of Venice* by Shakespeare you will have thought of this: what do we see of Shakespeare's own view, separate from the views he reflects of society, of African or Jewish people?

You may have studied *The Heart of Darkness* by Conrad, and if so you will have had the same discussion. In fact this is a text that often features on anthropology courses at university, precisely because it shows how literary texts can illustrate huge shifts in thinking in a society. What seemed liberal or forward looking at the time of writing seems limited and ethnocentric at a later date.

It is really important, then, for you to think carefully about context.

Social context

The world of film provides some very interesting parallels. To take one example, there were many "cowboy" or "western" films made in the 1950s, and they were enormously popular – simple plots in which the good guys - almost always the cowboys – beat the bad guys – almost always the "Indians." They tended to illustrate the thinking behind the well known quotation, "The only good Indian is a dead Indian." (This is attributed to General Sheridan during the War of Independence in the United States. In the context of the present day that quotation is of course absolutely unacceptable – even embarrassing.) Even though there were sometimes Native American characters who were on the "good" side, as scouts, perhaps, or messengers, these films reflected the status quo, the way society was for most people. The characters were types, the narrative reflected the cultural views of the powerful majority. There was no reflection of the systematic persecution that the Native Americans had been subjected to at the hands of the European immigrants. (This came later, as the knowledge of historical events became widespread.) The "American dream" was reinforced by showing that the good guys win – by defeating anyone who gets in the way – and by reinforcing the pride people could have in their predecessors who braved all dangers to make the country great. It was assumed that this was the only view there could be, and that the audience shared it.

These films were made for a general audience; they did not ask any serious questions, or upset the status quo; they created a feel-good factor that contributed to the post war recovery period. However, at the time they were being made, the civil rights movement was beginning to gain momentum, and this certainly did ask serious questions – about human rights, equality, citizenship, power. The 1950s also saw the beginning of the Cold War, and the polarisation of power and politics between East and West, with the fear both sides had of each other. It was a decade during which people were fervently discouraged from thinking independently, and during which, under Senator McCarthy, people who expressed views different from those of the government risked imprisonment, loss of livelihood or other persecution. Arthur Miller, who may be included in your study, was one of these. In one of his most widely known plays, *The Crucible,* he uses an historical parallel to condemn the persecution of liberals at the time; in another, *Death of a Salesman,* he questions the unthinking pursuit of the materialistic so-called "American dream." If you have studied either of these plays, you will know that, while you can understand them as tragedies without detailed knowledge of their contexts, you can only appreciate their subtlety and complexity – you will only get the whole picture – if you understand the social climate that inspired them.

When you include this perspective in approaching the "cowboy" films of the 1950s and early 1960s, you begin to see that what seemed like simple entertainment was as "political" in not questioning prevailing opinion as those that did. Your understanding of the text becomes much more sophisticated when you realise that part of the text is its context.

Context, then, is a very important aspect of your critical analysis, and it has different aspects.

Historical context

With some texts the relevance of context is obvious – for example, during a period of war, you can expect films and other media texts to encourage patriotism; and it is obvious that the characters of the enemies will reflect negative stereotypes – we have to hate the enemy or we will lose the war. The same is true of literary texts, whether they are poems, plays, novels or short stories – acknowledging this will help you to explain the use of stereotypes in the work, for instance. It will also be worthy of comment when you read something that seems to challenge this view. The poetry of Wilfred Owen, a British poet who died in the First World War, overflows with sorrow and angry condemnation of the people who believe there is anything good about sending young men to their death. In the context of the same war – but opposing sides – so does the German novelist Erich Maria von Remarque in *All Quiet On the Western Front;* this novel makes the same criticisms. The understanding you gain from knowing how and why these texts came from the circumstances in which they were written helps you to appreciate better the authors' use of imagery, narrative and stylistic features, their choice of genre and their purpose.

Cultural context

In addition to the historical and social contexts we have just looked at, the English A: Language and Literature course places a significant emphasis on cultural context. This has been alluded to already, but in Part Three it has a special focus, seen in the requirement that at both higher level and standard level one of the chosen texts must be read in translation and selected from the PLT. One of the reasons for this is to ensure that you recognise and think about the cultural assumptions you bring with you when reading a text. Works arising from cultures you are not familiar with can seem especially difficult because ideas or points of view you either don't share or haven't thought of may be taken for granted. Reading such works may require some cultural orientation or flexibility, and you have to remember that if you find the text in translation challenging or difficult, the challenge or difficulty is likely to arise from what you bring with you from your own cultural perspective rather than being part of the text you are studying. Writers don't usually write primarily for people from other cultures – they write within and for their own culture, to share the experience of life from its point of view, with its history and social norms. The reader needs to be equipped to understand the text; the challenge is to the reader. This is true of any literature, in any language, and in any culture.

Another reason there is a requirement to read at least one work in translation is that it shows how literature is a part of all cultures, all human experience. All human beings experience tragedy, whatever their culture and wherever they live; all human beings find humour in life's events. Literature is a way of sharing this and is part of all traditions, whether oral or written, formal or informal. Reading the literature of a culture gives an insight into how that culture works, and it is one of the benefits of this course that it nurtures such an understanding. This understanding will be reflected in your response in Paper 2.

Texts

What is a text?

Parts Three and Four focus specifically on literature, so a text here is a literary work written either in prose or in verse. It includes drama, poetry, literary fiction – the novel and the short story – as well as literary non-fiction. The Prescribed List of Authors, (PLA) clarifies this, and you should use it to check that you do know what genres your texts belong to. Sometimes students attribute works they are writing about to the wrong genre (or even just call a work a "book"!) and though this seems a trivial slip, it actually means that they have overlooked the conventions of the genre – a significant omission.

The text and the exam essay

When you prepare for Paper Two, your most important task is to know the literary works you have read and studied on your course very well. Simply being able to say more or less what happens in the story is not enough. You need to be able to analyse your texts, not just summarise them or refer to them in general. You need to be able to back up any point you make by referring very closely to a relevant extract, episode, stanza, line, scene; you need to be able to quote appropriately as well – nothing demonstrates your thorough familiarity with a text as effectively as a well chosen quotation. As you will probably have found when writing essays during the course, in most texts there are a few quotations that illustrate many of the points you want to make –sometimes as few as four or five, perhaps; these are the sort you need to learn. Keep them short; in exam conditions you won't have time to write out long ones.

In your study of your chosen works, you will have looked at different aspects of the whole, separating them from each other in order to understand how they fit together. When you do this, you are developing your critical understanding of the work, and this is what Paper Two assesses. The following paragraphs address some of these aspects, and should be read alongside the notes you will have made while studying your works. They list the main points you need to think about, but the list is not exhaustive. Seen as a list in this way, they should remind you of what you need to think about when you unpack an exam essay question.

Narrative

Whether you are considering a novel, short stories, a play, a biography or other literary non-fiction, there will be a narrative thread. It is, at its most basic, the "story." This is what underpins the work – whatever the writer's aims, the narrative is what holds the ideas together, and it has to be convincing. That is not to say that we have to believe, for instance, that the extraordinary events that take place in works in the genre of magical realism, really take place; it means that within the context of the work itself, the characters and events are believable. Detailed knowledge of the narrative will help you to address the themes and ideas; the narrative is the vehicle for the theme. Read your texts several times, so you are completely familiar with the plot and how it develops. The author's ideas are encapsulated in the way the narrative develops and concludes.

Character

Just as the narrative is a construct of the writer, so are the characters; the decisions they make, the things they say, their feelings, thoughts and actions – everything about them is designed by the author to reflect on or develop the ideas the work is focusing on. The characters have to be credible, like the narrative, for the writer's ideas to convince the reader or audience. When you write critically about characters you will find that you look at what they say, think and feel; what they do or don't do; and what is said about them by other characters. You will find that this is a rich source of quotations for any essay. These show us the author's ideas and intentions – in fact, the themes.

You may like or dislike a character; in your analysis you must show what makes that character likeable or unlikeable – how has the author created the reader's response, and why? Are the words used to describe this character emotive (producing an emotional response in the reader), stereotypical, factual, objective? Which other characters like/dislike this one, and what effect does that have on the reader? How do we know that this character reflects the views of the author? How, therefore, does the character contribute to our overall understanding of the author's themes? How does the author ensure that the reader sympathises in the required way, for or against, the various characters? To answer these questions you will need to go back to the relevant work and find the quotation that proves or illustrates the point. Either identify it in your copy of the text or write down the reference in your notes, and learn it; in the exam you will need to use this sort of evidence.

Narrative voice – who is telling the story?

In a prose text – a novel or short story – the voice of the narrator can be an important consideration. The "story" can be told from various different points of view, and these are part of the writer's means of conveying her or his themes. Sometimes the story is told by the author, who is outside of the action, thus seeing everything that happens and knowing what the characters are thinking; the term "omniscient author" is sometimes used to describe this. Sometimes the narrator of the story (not the author) is one of the characters, so the reader sees the narrative from a particular point of view – the author's view still, but conveyed differently, and without the possibility of knowing what all the other characters are thinking. Sometimes the narrative voice will change throughout the work, so different parts of story will be recounted by different characters – this enables the author to convey different points of view with equal weight.

Writers use many different devices to tell their narrative from various points of view and from the perspective of more than one character – that is, using different narrative different voices. These include diary entries and letters; you may have studied a work constructed as a series of letters, or extracts from a journal. Another way of exploring different perspectives on an issue is to give the same piece of narrative to two or more of the characters and let them tell it from their point of view. Mahfouz, an Egyptian author on the PLT, does this in his novel *Miramar*, and effectively creates for the reader a sense of the turmoil that accompanied the period of political upheaval and change.

You won't always need to comment on the narrative voice, but don't forget to think about it; it is often one of the devices a writer uses to explore a theme.

Stylistic features

Although the specific assessment of your understanding of the use of stylistic features in literary writing takes place in the Internal Assessment, especially in the Individual Oral Commentary (IOC), the use and effect of stylistic features is one of the assessment criteria for Paper Two, and so must be considered here as well.

The choices writers make about the way they write and language devices they use can have a substantial effect on the way the audience receives and understands a work. You will have noticed yourself, if you have ever read a prose text written in the present tense, that there is an impact on the narrative development; it create a limiting time frame. For example, if the narrative voice is that of one of the characters who speaks in dialect, or uses very colloquial language, this can affect the way you understand and relate to that character. The use of a very formal or very informal register can greatly affect the way you respond to the work. Some modern writers, aiming to make their work realistic, include swearing, while others avoid such a device. You may react quite strongly to this sort of language use. Some writers include lots of description of places, so you can see them imaginatively. Some writers habitually write in long sentences, like the American Henry James in his late nineteenth century novels, while others make their sentences short, like the Swedish Henning Mankell in his late twentieth century detective stories.

Choice of style in language use clearly plays its part in the personal response of the reader. If and when you write about this aspect of a work you need to think carefully about the writer's reasons for choosing to write this way.

Themes

The ideas a work develops, its message for the reader, the purpose for which it was written, the concerns it explores – all these make up its themes. It is the narrative that forms the framework within which they can be explored, and the characters who bring it to life; and of course they work as a whole rather than as separate items on a list. When we talk or write critically about literary texts, though, we have to think about the elements that make up the whole. That is the only way we can explain what a text means, or account for its effect, and you will have been learning how to approach texts in this way throughout you course. Think about context again, and you will see how important it is when you consider theme – the novel criticising war; the play describing political repression; the poetry condemning false patriotism. In these, as in most literary texts, something about the context in which they were written suggests the themes they deal with, either directly or indirectly. The theme is the idea, whether it is a specific issue or a more general consideration, that the author wants to present to the reader.

Shakespeare's *Romeo and Juliet* illustrates this. Shakespeare engages the audience with his tense story of how two young lovers, innocent and idealistic, full of optimism, plan to marry each other and thus end the generation long feud between their families. One by one their plans are destroyed by the petty jealousy and competitiveness of their families; finally, when Romeo and Juliet have run out of possible solutions, they commit suicide. Their parents are overcome with sorrow, realise that it is their fault, and agree to end their feud.

That, rather simply, is the narrative. Shakespeare even tells us how the story is going to end in the prologue. On its own, it does not explain Shakespeare's main idea, or theme. Told briefly in this way it is not even particularly sad, and yet of course the play is overwhelmingly tragic. The themes are delivered in a variety of ways, which include:

- Convincing, credible characters.
- The creation of minor characters that are recognisable and credible types.
- The quality of innocent optimism of the two main characters, which seems real enough for their death to feel truly moving.
- The use of imagery.
- Language that sparkles with wit.
- Quick verbal humour.
- The intensification of tragedy through verbal humour and humorous episodes.
- Believable examples of human weakness.
- The timeless relevance of themes. For example, when he describes what he calls "civil strife," or violence within society, audiences across time recognise the relevance of his theme. Similarly, diverse audiences can relate to his recurrent allusion to the timeless philosophical question of whether human beings have free will or are ruled by destiny.
- His narrative; the story of the "star cross'd lovers" is engaging, making his audience share his wish for a peaceful, cohesive society.
- The power of gangs in situations of urban deprivation.
- The fast pace and unremitting tension maintain audience attention.

These are some of the ways Shakespeare presents his themes to the audience – it is not exhaustive, and it is not detailed. It shows how the story and the all the other features of the play depend on each other and fit together. It demonstrates how we access the meaning of the play and account for its effect. Quotations illustrating all these points would be easy to find, so long as you knew the play well, and they would show your good understanding of the themes.

Language

One of the assessment criteria for Paper Two is Language, as with Paper One, and just as in Paper One the examiner will be looking for grammatical accuracy, correct sentence structure, appropriate vocabulary and formal style in your written English. You will be expected to use the appropriate technical terms for the stylistic features you discuss in your essay – the glossary at the end will serve as a reminder of these; it would be impossible to write a good literature essay without the relevant vocabulary. The list is fairly comprehensive, and you won't need to know all the terms – but you will need a solid core of critical vocabulary.

What is the content of Part Three?

If you are studying the course at standard level you will read two works, and at higher level, three. This is outlined in the assessment overview in chapter 1.

One of these works must be studied in translation, chosen from the Prescribed Literature in Translation list (PLT) at both higher and standard levels; this is to enable you to understand the way literature reflects the human condition wherever it is written spoken, sung, performed or in any way communicated; and in whatever culture it arises from, however different that is from the one you are familiar with. Hopefully it will help you to see what preconceptions you bring from your own culture when you read a literary work, probably unknowingly – if you find a work strange or surprising, it is worth asking yourself if it would seem strange or surprising to a person from the culture in which it was written. It probably wouldn't; that is why part three of the course puts such emphasis on **context,** and we will return to this.

Another of the texts you study for Paper Two, – the second and only other if you are following the course at standard level – can be chosen either from the PLA or freely, and must be written in English (in English for the purposes of this revision guide; it has to be written in the language studied); this gives the flexibility necessary to ensure that the literary texts can be studied within the context of the whole course, fitting the topics appropriately. They don't have to be separate from the study of other text types and topics.

At higher level, one text must be chosen from the PLT, one from the PLA, and the third can be chosen from either of these lists, or freely.

How will I be assessed?

There are five assessment criteria at both higher level and standard level for Paper Two. Each gains a maximum of five points, so the total is twenty five.

Assessment at standard level

The five assessment criteria look for the following:

- How well your answer shows that you know and understand your Part Three works and their contexts.

- How well you have understood what the question is asking, and how well you answer it.

- How aware you are that the writers' use of stylistic features adds to the meaning of their works, and how well you reflect your understanding of their effects.

- How organised and coherent your essay is.

- How accurately you write grammatically; how appropriate your style is for a formal essay; how effectively you use critical vocabulary.

The descriptors for the highest marks require you to be very good in response to these criteria.

Assessment at higher level

The five assessment criteria look for the following:

- Good knowledge and understanding your part three works and of the significance of their contexts.

- Good understanding of the implications of the question you have chosen reflected in an essay that addresses them; a good level of critical analysis.

- A thorough understanding of the use and effect of stylistic features in your chosen texts, and of how they add to your understanding of the work.

- A coherently planned and written answer to the question, with a logical development of ideas.

- Grammatical accuracy, formal register and style, appropriate use of critical vocabulary.

The descriptors for the highest marks require you to demonstrate excellence in these criteria.

What will the Paper Two exam look like?

- At both higher and standard levels Paper Two carries 25% of the total marks, and the maximum mark is twenty five.

- At standard level Paper Two is one and a half hours long.

- At higher level Paper Two is two hours long.

- There will be six possible essay questions.

- The questions for Paper Two are the same at standard level as at higher level; they are different every year, but the same for both levels.

NOTE: If you are taking the course at standard level you may be wondering how that can be right – it must make it easier to have two hours if the questions are the same. However, the questions are the same because the ideas about the function and purpose of literature that inform this course are, the same whatever the level. You will have the same discussions about texts, contexts, themes and style during the course. The difference between the levels lies in the number of texts you read – one more at higher level – and in what is expected of you in the exam.

At standard level you will not be expected to write with the same depth or level of complexity as those who take the course at higher level. This is reflected in the different grade descriptors for the assessment criteria at standard level. It is also reflected in the different lengths of time allocated.

Paper Two – some questions answered

How many questions will I have to answer?

Out of the six possible questions, you will have to answer one.

How many texts do I have to write about?

Two. The question will incorporate the instruction that you should respond in the light of two of your texts.

Do I have to compare the texts?

No. The questions will require you to write about two of your Part Three works, but you do not have to compare them. You may feel that the best way to answer the question you have chosen actually *is* to compare your texts, and if so then you should do so. You may, on the other hand, decide that comparison would not add value to your argument, in which case you should not compare the texts. You will not gain marks for writing comparatively, nor will you lose marks if you don't. You will gain marks for the organisation of your structure and the coherence of your argument, whether your essay compares two texts or writes about them separately in response to the question.

Will the questions be on my specific texts?

No. Your texts will not be named, but your answer has to be very specific to them. The question you choose in your exam will be the one you think is most appropriate for your texts, the one that lends itself most readily to exploration of their themes. As you read through the six questions, apply each one to your works – there will probably be one where you think there is nothing to say in response – it is completely irrelevant to your works; or you can apply it to one and not the other. Do not worry about this – simply move on to the next question. The questions are designed to pick up on broad aspects of literary works, their purpose and function, so most of them would be applicable to most works. You will choose the "best fit," the one you think gives you the most to say.

As soon as you have made your choice, you should change the question in your mind, so that instead of saying *"... with reference to two texts you have studied…"* you think of it as (for example) *"…with reference to Miramar by Mahfouz and The Crucible by Miller…"* This very basic ploy will help you to stay focused on your texts and not digress into generalisations. One thing you must never do is to write generally; you need to show detailed knowledge of the works.

What will the questions be like?

The questions will reflect the ideas about different aspects of context, literary devices and the way they work together to create the meaning of a work, described earlier in this chapter. They will not all require you to write about all of these aspects – all literary works differ, and the relevance of context, for instance, will be greater in some than in others. In all works, though, whatever the theme or context, the stylistic and literary choices the writer makes are critically significant, and you should always consider these elements.

Sometimes a question will include a quotation about life or literature and ask you to apply it to your two texts; others may ask you a direct question about the function or purpose of literature; yet others will focus particularly on literary and stylistic features; some will require you to address the cultural role of literature. You could also be asked to consider how the meaning and interpretation of a work is influenced by what the reader brings – another aspect of context.

Examples of possible questions

Here are some examples to show you how these questions could be phrased:

1. "The function of literature is to entertain – it cannot be taken seriously." Referring to texts you have studied, explain to what extent you agree with this comment.
   (You will obviously not agree!)

2. With reference to two works you have studied, show how important the narrative voice is in contributing to the way themes are understood.

3. Can a literary work written in one cultural, historical or social context be relevant in another, completely different context? Refer to two texts you have studied in your answer.

It would be good practice to try planning all of these, relevant to the works you have studied for Part Three.

To sum up, the exam questions will expect you to be able to discuss how meaning is created in your two texts through social, cultural, historical and political context; the critical context in which it is read; and the use the writers make of literary and stylistic devices.

By showing that you can do this, you demonstrate the learning outcomes for Part Three.

You can see an example of a Paper Two on page 60 with a sample student response and examiner's comments.

What are the learning outcomes for Part Three?

These have been referred to briefly already, in Chapter Two.

The course should enable you to:

- Consider the significance of social, cultural, historical, political context on the way a work is understood. You may have examined this in texts that arise from a period of political oppression, for example *The Crucible* by Arthur Miller, written during the era of Senator McCarthy; or of war, like *Black Rain* by Ibuse; or in any work reflecting ideas about different social groups, the individual and society, religious conflict, aspects of culture – whatever the theme and narrative, the context will be an important part of the meaning.

- Show you understand that the use of stylistic features in a text, including choice of genre and structure, constitute part of its meaning; and that these can also be influenced by context. You will have discussed this when exploring formal aspects of your works like the use of literary or poetic language, characterisation, narrative, style and structure.

- Understand that the attitudes and values of the writer and those of the context in which she or he is writing – which may be different – have an influence on the way the reader receives and understands a work; that a work may therefore be understood in different ways at different times; and that the context of the reader can also influence the way a work is understood. You will have considered such points in your reading of literature in translation and from other cultures.

How do I plan the essay?

It is unlikely that candidates from different schools anywhere in the world will have studied the same set of texts – the PLA and the PBL are extensive, including a very wide range of texts from the accepted canon of literature to the less obvious, the more modern and the more varied. (Many of the texts written in earlier periods, that we think of as "literature" because they have stood the test of time and are still highly critically regarded, were, of course, "less obvious" and were certainly "modern" when they were written; you may well have engaged in discussion during the course about what makes a text literary and durable.) This means that advice about planning and structuring an essay cannot be text specific.

There are, however, some aspects to planning a literature essay, and general points to keep in mind, that apply to any title.

Planning points – The essay question

As we have seen, the questions will ask you to reflect on the aims of the course and on the learning outcomes. They will not specify your Part Three works by name, but will ask you to relate your answer to texts you have read for Part Three. When you have decided which question to answer, you need to work out exactly what it is asking. This is a really important step in planning the essay: if you leave it out you run the risk of not answering it fully, or including irrelevant material. The examiner assumes that you know the work – you don't have to prove it by writing everything you know about it; you will gain nothing by writing a summary of the narrative and listing the themes.

You have to show that you can select what is relevant in order to address the question; in order to do this you have to be clear about exactly what the question is asking. Start by breaking it down into its constituent parts – this is often referred to as "unpacking" the question. You can do this by asking yourself questions about the question.

Try it with this question:

Essay Question: How is our critical understanding of a work affected by cultural perspectives?

Question	Answer
What are the key terms or words?	Critical understanding; cultural perspectives
Which aspect of the course is it particularly referring to?	Context; culture; stylistic features
How are the different parts of the question connected?	One part of the question (reception of the work) has to be answered in the light of the other (understanding of context).
Can it be rephrased without losing or changing its meaning?	When we read a literary work, the fact that we belong to our own culture influences how we understand and interpret the ideas from a different culture in that work.

What should I include in the introduction?

This needs to name your texts – not just by listing them, but by incorporating their titles neatly into a sentence. For example, by saying, "X by Some One and Z by Someone Else are both examples of works arising from a cultural context the reader needs to understand in order to critically appreciate the writer's ideas." The introduction should reflect your understanding of the question and indicate how you will answer it – the line you will take. This is the place to include your rewording of the question. It shows that you know what you are being asked and indicates that you will address it.

How should I organise my ideas in the main body?

There are various ways of organising your ideas for this.

You are writing about two works, so you need to apply the question to both of them. You don't have to write comparatively, so you may only need a link transitional sentence; but if you feel that a comparative response is more appropriate, you will probably want to reflect this in your plan.

Some people work well with "spider diagrams," with the question at the centre and all the ideas it gives rise to coming out from it; others work from lists of ideas, already thinking in paragraphs or sections.

The really important thing is to take into account the different parts of the question, relating them to both texts. Your plan, however you feel comfortable with it, needs to reflect on how the question is relevant to the text, with supporting textual evidence – that is, quotations. The quotations are usually the starting point. Very close reference to a specific episode, or description, or conversation can be a substitute for quotation, but in any text there will be short sentences or phrases you can remember easily – these will help to make your essay detailed.

Remember that although you will refer to the narrative in your essay, the point is to apply the question to it, not to summarise it. You might say "This play is about a poor family who mistakenly believes it can trust some rich fellow Kenyans," because it introduces a comment you want to make, but you will not recount the whole story. The examiner knows your texts so you don't have to retell them.

What should I include in the conclusion?

The conclusion, like the introduction, should be concise. You need to show that you have addressed the question, and sum up how you have answered it. You will need to include reference to the question and your introduction, as well as to a key point from the development of your ideas.

English A: Language and Literature

Paper Two – Texts and Contexts

Standard Level and Higher Level

Answer ONE of the following questions:

1. To what extent can literature be regarded as a useful means of political expression? Refer closely to two of the works you have studied in your answer.

2. "To read the literature is to understand the culture." Making close reference to at least two of the works you have studied for Part 3, explain whether you agree or disagree with this statement.

3. How important is the historical, social or political context of a literary work in relation to the reader's understanding of the themes? Refer in detail to two of the works you have studied in your answer.

4. "Literature is a candle lighted in the mind and left alight." Show how at least two of the works you have studied illustrate the truth of this quotation by referring closely to them.

5. How valid is literary fiction as a means of making social or political comment? In your answer, refer closely to two of the works you have studied.

6. How important are genre and the use of stylistic features to our understanding and appreciation of the author's purpose?

Paper 2, Number 3

Works of literature are often strongly influenced by the author's historical, political and social context which is why it is important to consider the context of a text in order to understand it. The plays The Crucible and Master Harold and the Boys both have a common theme of oppression, but due to their different historical, political and social contexts, they are also very different in several aspects.

Master Harold and the Boys was published during the South African period of Apartheid where the systematic human rights abuses of native South Africans were institutionalised by government forces. In order to show the devastating effects this political divide had on people's social relations, the author uses the characters of Hally, Wille and Sam, each of whom presents a different aspect of the issue. Hally is presented as a white South African that treats native South Africans differently but still respectfully unlike the other white characters mentioned in the play. Sam is an intelligent and relatively educated native South African who tries to maintain the friendly relationship with Hally throughout the play in order to overcome the racist discrimination used in his society, in at least one significant part of his life. Therefore the relationship of Sam and Hally and its development can be seen as one of the most important themes in this book, contributing to the overall message which is why it is important to analyse it with regard to the context of Apartheid. While Sam and Wille are servants of Hally and his family and hence are not treated as grown men, but like inferiors, there still is a friendly relationship between them and Hally which becomes visible when Hally demands to have his lunch served by them but still discusses his homework and opinions on history, and even philosophical topics such as the meaning of 'greatness' in a friendly and respectful manner.

Hally's and Sam's friendship is also symbolised by the flying of the kite; Hally recalls an event from his childhood in which he was flying a kite with the 'black man' Sam (which was socially unacceptable at the time) and feeling happiness and joy as a consequence of this. This event is described in such a way that it seems that racism was not an issue for Hally at this point in his life; this shows that Fugard is saying racism is not natural but artificial and constructed by society and its rules. Their relationship however drastically changes when Hally learns that his alcoholic and abusive father is about to come home. Being scared of his father and the social consequences his friendship with Sam and Willie could have, Hally accepts the role of the 'white man' and demands to be called 'Master Harold' rather than Hally, highlighting the strong contrast in social power and perceived superiority and inferiority. This becomes especially clear when Hally spits at Sam, saying "You can't fly a kite in the rain" showing that the former friendly relationship, symbolised by the flying of the kite, has changed permanently. This represents the destruction of natural human relationships by the institutional racism put in place by the South African government. While the social roles and their differences are very clear to a reader who has only read the play itself but has not learned about its context, the full message about the destructive nature of racist regimes like the Apartheid government cannot be understood without taking into account the social, historical and political context of the play. The characters in Master Harold and the Boys represent specific aspects and social groups of the oppressive system which can only be fully understood if the historical, political and social aspects of the Apartheid government are taken into account.

The Crucible is play published in North America during the time of McCarthyism, which was the idea that all attempts to spread communist or socialist ideas were anti-American and deserved to be punished. The threat of the Cold War and the negative sentiments towards the USSR led to a widespread hysteria and the persecution and large numbers of accusations against anyone who was suspected to have Communist ideas or political links, many of which had no basis other than this political hysteria. In The Crucible, the sixteenth century village of Salem and its citizens' obsession with witchcraft is used to show the dangers of theocracy and totalitarianism without directly mentioning the problems of McCarthyism. This can be seen when the characters, especially Hale, talk all the time about witchcraft and the devil and the way they accuse people like Tituba, John Proctor and his wife of witchcraft and communing with the devil, when they are actually all Christians. The theme of witchcraft is used because most readers of a modern time will not hold any of these beliefs themselves and this contributes to the perceived absurdity and hysteria of the situation.

Characters such as Danforth or Hawthorne who run the court in the play, represent the committee set up by McCarthy to try people for un-American activities, or even McCarthy himself, and are deliberately made to be unlikeable. They are the antagonists of the play while the victims of their judgements, John Proctor, his wife and numerous other people, are depicted as likeable characters even if they have some negative aspects (for instance John Proctor has an affair with Abigail Williams). John Proctor is described as an intelligent man and more insight is given into the feelings of the persecuted characters to make the readers empathise with them and their situation. The reader does not feel that their punishment is deserved but that they are victims of totalitarian ideas.

By using characters in this way the author aims to create an understanding of the general problems of totalitarianism in the readers which can contribute to a development towards personal rejection of a specific totalitarian system such as McCarthyism.

If the historical, political and social contexts were not known however, the reader could gain a general understanding of totalitarian systems, but the reason why the author uses a sixteenth century village rather than 1950s America would not be known. Since McCarthyism was employed very strongly by the USA to persecute celebrities and artists, the author could not address this problem directly during this period of time. In order to seemingly detach his political commentary from McCarthyism the town of Salem is chosen, and some old fashioned language devices are used to make it seem genuinely historical. This makes it seem as though McCarthyism is not being criticised while in fact it is being condemned indirectly. In order to understand this significant aspect of the play, some knowledge about the fear of communism and the danger of mass hysteria is required. Overall it can be said that both Master Harold and the Boys, and The Crucible were influenced by their political, social and historical contexts and that these contexts have to be understood in order to improve the reader's understanding of the themes in the texts. Master Harold and the Boys analyses the way relationships and friendships are destroyed by the institutional racism of Apartheid, using the characters of Sam, Willie and Hally. The Crucible indirectly criticises the totalitarian ideas of McCarthyism using the example of Salem and its witch hunt which, as in the other play, can be understood by readers in a much clearer way when the historical, political and social contexts are analysed.

Sample general examiner comment

After every examination session, examiner reports are written by examiners in every subject. These reports identify the overall strengths and weaknesses of candidate responses to a particular exam. Because they include an overview of mistakes that are very commonly made, they constitute a very useful revision tool. This sample set of comments makes reference to aspects relevant to all five assessment criteria for Paper Two; the points here do not refer to a specific examination paper. They identify areas that are frequently commented on by examiners, and are useful as an extra tool when you prepare for the exam.

- Candidates need to demonstrate closer knowledge of the individual texts. While most show they have read their works and know the narrative, there is very little quotation or close reference. Without this answers are too general. (criterion A)

- Candidates need to be familiar with the assessment criteria; these ask for critical appreciation and comment, not just generalised knowledge of the works. (criteria A and B)

- Most candidates demonstrate good basic understanding of the significance of context, but need to illustrate it with examples. (criterion A)

- Candidates need to show much closer, more detailed knowledge of the texts – too often exam scripts reflect little or no understanding of the use and effects of stylistic features. (criteria A and B)

- Too many candidates use an inappropriate register. Some write as though Paper Two called for a personal response, and use the first person; others are conversational, using an informal register; yet others write rhetorically, as though the essay could be the text of a speech. The use of an inappropriate register often results in a lack of balanced in the essay. (criterion D)

- There is little evidence of planning in the scripts of a significant number of candidates. A frequent consequence of this is lack of organisation. (criterion C)

- Candidates need use paragraphs to reflect the organisation and development of ideas. (criterion C)

- Many candidates fail to make appropriate use of the introduction to show that they understand the question and have taken into consideration all its different parts. This indicates incomplete understanding of the function of the introduction, and often results in either partial or incorrect answers. (criteria A, B and C)

Exam Preparation – some questions answered

The list of questions below sums up the key practical points you have to keep in mind when you write your essay for Paper Two. They apply to all essays, of course, but it is particularly important to remember them in exams – in timed conditions you have to be really focused on organising your knowledge and ideas relevantly and quickly. Most of these questions address the sort of points the examiners make in their reports when they have finished marking all their scripts and can see where candidates have gained and lost marks.

There is nothing here that you don't already know – the questions should simply remind you and help you to focus your thoughts on the practicalities of writing a literature essay.

Do I need to write out the whole question?

No; but while you don't need to write out the whole question for your answer, you must make sure you write the question number – don't leave the examiner to guess. However, writing the question can help you to keep it fully in mind, so you don't forget about part of it.

Should I refer to the question in my introduction?

Yes; you need to reflect it. Look at the different parts of the question and identify the key words. Is it asking you how **valid** some aspect of the works is? Is it asking you how **important context** is? Is it asking you to reflect on the **significance** of something? Use these words in your introduction to show that you have understood the question and will address it. They are the core of your answer.

How long should my introduction be?

Short. As we saw in the last answer, you need to reflect the question and use the key words you have identified, to show that you have understood what is being asked and that you will answer it. You need to name the works you are writing about, and say who wrote them, giving their name in full. Thereafter you can refer to the author by surname only (never refer to her or him by first name: Charles Dickens can be Dickens but never just Charles). Do not write a long, general introduction – focus straight away on the question.

Do I have to write formally?

Yes; do not write conversationally or colloquially – this is a formal essay. Do not use contractions like "don't".

Should I write in the first person?

No; the literature essay is formal; you must write impersonally. Writing in the first person is personal, and subjective. The convention is that you state critical facts objectively, with evidence; not that you give a series of personal opinions. For instance, you would not write (about Shakespeare's *Hamlet*: I think Hamlet is confused about the meaning of life when he says "To be or not to be, that is the question"

Instead you would write: Hamlet shows that he is confused about the meaning of life when he says "To be or not to be, that is the question."

Do I need a plan?

Yes; criterion D for Paper Two calls for logical development of your ideas, and for coherent structure of your essay. Without a plan these requirements are difficult to achieve; if you think of something you want to add, you have to resort to margin or footnotes, or even to writing paragraphs at the end and directing the examiner to them. Your structure is compromised – your thinking is unclear.

A plan doesn't need to be very detailed; but you do need to write down the main points you want to include, and the order in which you want to address them. Note the quotations you want to use to illustrate your points. Having a plan will ensure that you think about the logical structure of your response.

Do I have to compare the two works?

No; you have to apply the question to two works, and you may compare them if you feel that comparison is useful. You will neither gain marks by comparing texts nor lose them if you don't. If you think that your answer will be better if you include an element of comparison, then by all means do so – but you do not have to. Don't force it in unnecessarily. Unless you choose to compare your two works, you should write about each work separately. If you do find you want to compare them in some ways, then you should write about the aspects you are comparing in turn, rather than writing about one text and then the other.

Should I summarise the narrative or plot?

No; the examiner does not want you to show that you know the story – that is assumed. Only outline as much of the narrative as you need to answer the question. Resist the temptation to include everything you know about the work! Hopefully you will know a great deal more than you need, so pick and choose; use only what is relevant to the focus of your question.

Do I really have to use technical words?

Yes; of course you won't just throw in long words for the sake of it, but if you are writing about a *novel*, don't call it a *book*. Refer to the *narrative* rather than the *story*. If you are writing about comedy, learn the different types so you can write precisely. Make sure you know the names of the different genres. The person who writes plays is a *playwright*, while prose fiction and literary non-fiction are written by an *author,* in the same way that the person who writes poetry is a *poet.* These are very basic, and you will find more in the glossary at the end – it should help you to revise the vocabulary you have learned during the course.

Is it necessary to learn quotations?

Yes; you MUST show that your knowledge of your works is detailed. You do this by referring to a very specific section of the work, or by quoting from it, to support your ideas. Every time you make one of your main points, you must evidence it in this way. The quotations you learn by heart will be short, and you will probably find that you only need five or six for each text – but you cannot demonstrate detailed knowledge of your works without them.

What should I write in the conclusion?

You have to show that you have answered the question. You will refer back to the question itself, to how you said in your introduction that you would address it, and what you have concluded or shown. Don't worry if you haven't concluded anything definite – the questions on Paper Two, as you can see from the sample paper at the end of this chapter, often ask you to consider texts in the light of an idea, or they may ask you how far your works illustrate a concept; in answers to such questions, your conclusion will sum up your reflections and give an overview of your argument rather than agreeing or disagreeing, or giving a yes/no answer.

An examiner might also tell you to:

- Make sure that you reflect the development of your ideas and the effectiveness of your structure by using paragraphs.

- Indent new paragraphs – that is, start writing a little way in from the margin, so the new paragraph is visible.

- Check that you have presented quotations correctly.

Chapter Four

External Assessment – Written tasks

Introduction to the written tasks

At both higher level and standard level you are required to complete written tasks that reflect in an imaginative way your response to the different parts of the course. Papers One and Two and the Internal Assessment allow you, through your critical analysis of various texts, to show your understanding of the ways that audience, purpose and context affect the way language conveys meaning. The written tasks demonstrate the same understanding by showing that you can use language effectively yourself to convey meaning with a specific purpose, in a particular context, and for a defined audience.

Standard level requirements

At standard level you are required to complete three written tasks, with rationales, and to submit one of them. Each written task must arise from a different part of the course; at least one written task must relate to part one or part two, and at least one must be based on a literary text from part three or part four. The content and nature of the task is described after the outline of the higher level requirements.

Higher level requirements

The requirements at higher level are different, in that you have to submit two written tasks. One, task 1, is the imaginative response required at standard level; at higher level you complete four of these, and submit one, with a rationale. Each task must relate to a different part of the course. The nature of this task is described in the next section.

You are required to complete a second task as well; whereas task 1 is an imaginative response, task 2 is a formal essay, a critical response to one of six pre-set questions. You do not write a rationale for this second task, but instead you include an outline. The next section addresses these requirements in more detail.

What do the written tasks consist of?

Task 1

This is your opportunity to write in the style of some of the text types you have studied. The choice of text type is yours – you have complete control over this, and should enjoy it – it is intended to be imaginative, so have some fun. Show that you know how campaigns can call us to action by arousing feelings of pity, or anger; or show that you, too, know how to make a holiday destination desirable; or imagine that you are a journalist reporting on an environmental disaster. The form of the written task can be that of any of the many text types you have read and studied in all four parts of the course and will reflect on or arise from your topics. You must not write an essay – you write essays in Paper One and Paper Two – but you can choose other text types according to your planned purpose, context and audience.

This is your work, and is not set by your teacher. The teacher's role is to guide you in your choice of task, discussing your ideas and giving you feedback on your first draft.

What is the rationale?

You will have to write a rationale when you complete your written task explaining:

- How it is connected to the part of the course it arises from.
- What specific aspect(s) of the course your task reflects on or develops.
- What sort of task it is and how you have reflected this in your language and style choices.
- Who the audience is, what your purpose is, and what is important about the context.

You can see from these points that the purpose of the rationale is to show that your use of language is based on your knowledge of what makes it effective – that you understand the connection between the choices you make when you use language and how effectively you convey the meaning you intend. The rationale is short – you will find it challenging to say all you want to about your purpose and how you tried to achieve it in 200 to 300 words. You will have to leave out anything unnecessary, making only the important points – be focused and precise, and make sure you do address all four points.

When you are planning your written tasks, you should keep these points in mind, and not start drafting your work until you have thought about them in relation to your idea. They are very specific, and if you don't think about them until after your finish the task, the "fit" is not likely to be very good. Use the points in the rationale to guide your planning.

When your work is sent off for external assessment, the task itself and the rationale will be accompanied by a cover sheet; this contains important information like your name and candidate number and your school name and centre number. It requires you to list the topics you have studied during the course for parts one and two, and the texts you have studied for parts three and four. You will have to identify the text type of your task; and you will also have to give the word count for both the task (between 800 and 1,000 words) and your rationale (between 200 and 300 words). Any text titles or topics mentioned in the rationale should cross reference with the course outline on your cover sheet.

Choosing a written task (task 1)

The balance between the literary and the non literary parts of the course is reflected in the requirement to complete written tasks for both; this does not mean that the task itself needs to be literary if the part of the course it relates to is literary; nor does it mean that you may not write in a literary genre for the task related to parts one or two. For instance, if you have read *Lord of the Flies* by William Golding in part three, you could write a police report about the events on the island in the story – that is, a non-literary text type – for your task; and if one of your topics is conflict, you could write a biography or a short story inspired by a documentary case study of a victim of war. In this case, since the text related to your task is a media text, and you will have looked at how the media influence people's understanding of events, you would place your task in part two. If, however, still working within the topic of conflict, you have read politicians' rhetorical speeches in times of war – Sir Winston Churchill in the UK during the Second World War, for instance, or Nelson Mandela speaking at his trial prior to his imprisonment on Robben Island – you might want to write a rhetorical speech by a political person about the evils of the arms trade and the recruitment of child soldiers. This would relate to part one.

You could write a speech, a letter, a diary entry, a campaign item, a legal report, a blog, a newspaper article, a film script, a ballad, a play, a short story, a pastiche, an opinion column – this list is not exhaustive. You will choose the text type because it suits your purpose and audience. Be clear about your purpose and audience – they will greatly influence the language and vocabulary you choose. Then think about the appropriate style – if it is a newspaper article, what stylistic features must you include that will characterise the text type of your task accurately? What is your message? How are you going to make this task demonstrate your understanding of how considerations such as audience, purpose, context, text type, presentation and other elements influence the way you can convey your meaning?

When you have thought about this, and discussed it with your teacher, you can start writing; your teacher can comment in general terms on your first draft, but may not annotate or mark it. It must be your own work, and you and your teacher will both have to sign a statement on your cover sheet to that effect.

Do I need to reference my sources?

Yes; any text or source you base your task on, such as an advertisement or newspaper report, or speech must be referenced in a bibliography. The same applies to any material you may have referred to or used in support of your ideas.

Task 2 – higher level only

Three areas of study are identified for Language A: Language and Literature, and they form the context for the questions for task 2. These relate to the topics, texts and ideas you have studied and reflected on in all four parts of the course.

They are:

Reader, culture and text – here you are reflecting on how our understanding of a text comes from our own cultural context: the meaning of a text comes not only from the person who produces it, but from the person who receives it – the reader – as well. So, just as a text is created within its own culture, period of time and social setting, a reader brings to a reading of the text her or his culture, social group, or period of time. Age, gender, language, ethnicity and other cultural groupings can all impact on the way a reader understands a text. You have considered such aspects of reading a text in all parts of the course, and the questions for this area of study invite you to explore these ideas. The work you have read from the PLT should illustrate this – that is why there is the requirement to read a text in translation. Equally, you may have read news reports or campaign items referring to issues like the death penalty, for instance, that reflect great cultural differences of perception.

Power and privilege – here you are thinking about how and why certain groups of people are reflected in particular ways in literary and non-literary texts; what groups are left out or presented as insignificant; and what this says about who is powerful and who is powerless in society. So you will consider the use of stereotypes and other devices to marginalise certain groups – think, for instance, about the way politicians and the media often portray refugees and asylum seekers, and how their choice of vocabulary and use of stylistic features reinforce the powerlessness of these groups. If you read President Obama's acceptance speech the first time he was elected as President of the United States, you see this in reverse – groups often omitted by politicians were included in this speech. President Obama addressed powerless, poor and minority groups especially because his intention was to include them, not to exclude them by leaving them out. The significance of what is included and what is omitted is relevant in many different text types and genres, in connection with many minority groups, as you will have seen in all four parts of the course.

Text and genre – here you are reflecting on genre. You have seen throughout the course that, for any genre, there are characteristic ways of using language, and choices of stylistic features – these are the *conventions* of a genre. For instance, you expect to find a greater use of imagery in poetry; of abbreviation in a text message; of rhetorical features in a speech; of persuasive language in an advertisement or campaign. This area of study invites you to think about the effect of these conventions of genres, and on the connection between genre or text type and audience, purpose and context. It also invites you to think about the effect of change of genre when a text is "translated" into a different genre; we are accustomed to seeing films based on novels, for instance – you may well have discussed what is lost and what is gained in that process. You almost certainly will have considered this if you have studied *The Crucible* by Arthur Miller, a particularly interesting example of genre shift since Miller directed the film. You may have read the novel *Wuthering Heights* by Emily Bronte, and listened to the popular song by Kate Bush.

For task 2, two questions have been devised for each of these areas of study, and you have to choose one as the focus of a critical response based on your studies during the course. The texts you select as the basis of your essay can be longer ones, like a novel or play; or shorter ones, like newspaper articles or letters. You can choose from any of the four parts of the course for task two, but you must remember that if you choose a literary base for task two, task one must be non-literary.

This is a formal essay, and must be structured accordingly, with an introduction, clearly developed ideas or line of argument, and a conclusion.

What are the questions for task 2?

Reader, culture and text

1. How could the text be read and interpreted differently by two different readers?
2. If the text had been written in a different time or place or language or for a different audience, how and why might it differ?

Power and privilege

1. How and why is a social group represented in a particular way?
2. Which social groups are marginalised, excluded or silenced within the text?

Text and genre

1. How does the text conform to, or deviate from, the conventions of a particular genre, and for what purpose?
2. How has the text borrowed from other texts, and with what effects?

These questions are as open as possible, to allow you to choose from the whole course; they avoid directing you towards literary texts, which, since you have studied them in depth might seem to be a safe choice. Whatever you choose, whether literary or non-literary, the important thing to understand is that your essay must be very specifically text focused and not general. Don't start planning your essay before you decide which text(s) you are going to apply to the question.

Before you decide, it is a good idea to consider all the questions in relation to the texts you have studied, and to identify the literary and non-literary texts that would be suitable for each; you will find that some questions lend themselves better to your non-literary texts, while others seem perfect for your literary works.

Just as with task 1, you can discuss your choice of question with your teacher, and receive guidance on your essay plan. When the essay is complete, you will write your outline and complete the relevant sections of your cover sheet; your signature guaranteeing the authenticity of your work for task 1 applies to task 2 as well.

Assessment of the written tasks

How will I be assessed?

The written tasks are worth 20% of the total mark allocation. This means that at standard level the single task carries the full 20%, while at higher level each of the two tasks carries 10%. For task 1, though the criteria are the same at higher and standard, the level descriptors are different, reflecting the different expectations. The criteria for task 2 are different from those for task 1, reflecting the difference in the nature of the tasks.

The assessment criteria

To summarise these for task 1: at both levels, your task has to show that you understand the topic, that you understand that different text types use language and stylistic features differently and so have their own conventions of usage, that you have organised and structured your task well, that you have used language effectively and style and register appropriately. In addition, that you have written a rationale that reflects your understanding of the topic, and shows how you have demonstrated this in your written task.

Standard level

Criterion A – Rationale

This criterion assesses the extent to which you have explained successfully how your task is linked to the aspect of the course you are exploring.
Marks available: 2

Criterion B – Task and content

This criterion assesses the extent to which your task shows that you understand the topic or topics you have based it on; how appropriately you have matched the content to your task; and how effectively you use the conventions of your chosen text type to show that you understand them.

To gain marks in the top range, you need to show good understanding of the topic(s) or text(s) you have chosen, consistently match you content appropriately to your text, and show good understanding of the conventions of your text type.
Marks available: 8

Criterion C – Organisation

This criterion asks how organised your task is and how coherently it is structured.

To gain marks in the top range, your task needs to be well organised and coherently structured.
Marks available: 5

Criterion D – Language and style

This criterion assesses the extent to which your use of language is accurate and your style is effective; and how appropriate your choice of register is to your task.

To gain marks in the top range, the language and style of your task need to be effective and the register appropriate to your task.
Marks available: 5

Higher level

Task 1

Criterion A – Rationale

This criterion assesses the extent to which you have explained successfully how your task is linked to the aspect of the course you are exploring.
Marks available: 2

Criterion B – Task and content

This criterion assesses the extent to which your task shows that you understand the topic or topics you have based it on; how appropriately you have matched the content to your task; and how effectively you use the conventions of your chosen text type to show that you understand them

To gain marks in the top range you have to show excellent understanding of the topic or text(s); match content to task appropriately throughout; show excellent understanding of the conventions of your text type.
Marks available: 8

Criterion C – Organisation

This criterion asks how organised your task is and how coherently it is structured.

To gain marks in the top range your task has to be effectively organised, with a coherent and effective structure.
Marks available: 5

Criterion D – Language and style

This criterion assesses the extent to which your use of language and style is effective; and how appropriate your choice of register and style is to your task.

To gain marks in the top range your language needs to show a very good degree of accuracy: good sentence construction and vocabulary; confident style and effective register.
Marks available: 5

Task 2

In summary, your essay must be a well organised, coherently structured critical response, with effectively developed ideas supported by well chosen references to your chosen text(s.) It must be written in language that is accurate, clear and effective, with good sentence structure and appropriate style and register. This breaks down as follows:

Criterion A – Outline

This criterion assesses the extent to which your outline highlights clearly the focus of your task.
Marks available: 2

Criterion B – Response to the question

This criterion asks to what extent your essay shows that you understand the expectations of the question you have chosen; how relevant and focused your response is to these expectations; and how well you support your ideas with well chosen references to the text.
Marks: 8

Criterion C – Organisation and argument

This criterion assesses your task on how well it is organised, how coherently it is structured, and how well developed your argument is.
Marks available: 5

Criterion D – Language and style

This criterion assesses the effectiveness of your language and style, and how appropriately you have chosen register.
Marks available: 5

Sample written task

The programme summary on the cover sheet for this task would show that texts in all four parts addressed the topic of racism.

The task summary on the cover sheet would state the word count for the rationale and for the written task. It would also identify the text type.

Speech on the occasion of the 10th anniversary of Stephen Lawrence's death

Okey Ndibe once said: "a story that must be told never forgives silence." One story that must be told began ten years ago, on April 22nd 1993. It's a story, a true story, that, because of the immense crime it tells, is still hard to believe. It has become a very familiar story, a story that has filled every one of us with rage and disgust, if not desperation. It's a story of immense evil, and injustice. Today, we commemorate the victims of this story and the immeasurable pain it's caused – the story of Stephen Lawrence's murder.

The story begins at a bus stop on Well Hall road, in Eltham, in South East London. It was from here that Stephen Lawrence ran away from five white racists. While he was waiting for the bus they came across the road and stabbed him. They killed him with two heave blows from their knives. Because he was black.

An appalling story, a horrible story, a disgusting story so far. The next chapter begins with the first police officers arriving at the scene. They didn't just see a bleeding body, they saw a bleeding black body. Stephen's gross injuries were simply ignored.

The police officers who dealt with Stephen Lawrence's murder did not act quickly. Even during the vital hours directly after the murder, there was no direction. Many officers were involved – but they just didn't do their job. If they had, Stephen's murderers would have been arrested within days. Instead, there was poor surveillance of the suspects' homes. Witnesses who approached the police were not taken seriously – Duwayne Brooks for example. He was Stephen's friend, and was with him when the murder happened. He was neither considered a primary victim of the attack, nor a primary witness. His repeated formal identifications of Luke Knight and Neal Acourt, two of the killers, were simply not considered. Three of the main suspects were finally arrested on the 7th of May – more than a fortnight after the murder. And 15 days is a very long time to destroy evidence and inhibit potential witnesses.

This story goes on and on like this – there is the part about the completely ineffective search of the suspects' homes, about the crucial lack of documentation and records, about the discharge of the five suspects, and so on... everything that could have gone wrong in this investigation did go wrong. So is this just a story about police incompetence?

The officers from the Metropolitan Police Service were certainly incompetent – but they would have shown their competence had Stephen Lawrence been white. Racism undermined the whole investigation. There can be no doubt about that. But Stephen Lawrence's story has shown us, too, that the symptoms of racism are not always easy to recognise. Subtle racism is as hideous as overt racism. The flaws in the police investigation provide shocking evidence of this, as does the behaviour of the officers.

Inspector Groves, for example, was one of the first to arrive at the scene of the murder. He assumed that there had been a fight. The bleeding person on the ground was not a victim to him, but a potential offender. The other black boy on the scene, Duwayne Brooks, was not treated as a victim of the attack. His integrity was blatantly questioned. What he said was not believed. He was asked several times if he was sure the attack had been unprovoked. Imagine you were asked a question like this after your best friend was just murdered before your eyes! Duwayne was treated like a suspect, and not like a victim.

The other obvious victims of the attack, Stephen's parents, were not treated as such either. Family Liaison failed to establish a link of trust and competence between the police and Mr and Mrs Lawrence.

We also know about the use of offensive language. Stephen and Duwayne were often referred to as the "two coloured lads". What seems most significant though is the fact that many officers simply refused to accept that the motive for Stephen's murder was purely racism. This was not only the case during the first couple of days: many officers continued to believe that Stephen's skin colour didn't make a difference to his five killers – although we know that the first and probably the only thing they said to Stephen was "What, what nigger!" Ignorance of racism is as lethal as racism itself.

When the investigation into a racist killing is infected with racism itself justice can't possibly be done. One year after Stephen's murder the Crown Prosecution Service refused to prosecute his five killers because of "insufficent evidence to take action against any individual." The Lawrence's private prosecution collapsed as well. It was only when the McPherson Inquiry was launched in 1998 that some justice could be done. The mistakes made by the police were laid bare, and their main cause was named: racism.

Stephen Lawrence's story is not just the story of a racist murder, but the story of a racist society. Stephen was buried in Jamaica – his parents felt that he could never find peace in a country where black people have to put up with so much hatred. We see signs of racism every day, everywhere. Stephen Lawrence's story has made this painfully clear. So, ten years after Stephen Lawrence's murder, we still have to put up with ignorance and racism, whether subtle or overt.

But while the story of Stephen Lawrence's murder has taught us how lethal and destructive racism is, it has also shown us that there are many people like us, people who want justice; for Stephen, for his parents and for society. Doreen and Neville Lawrence's campaign for justice has been supported by a huge number of people, black and white. We cannot prevent the genesis of racism, but we can fight its spread – by telling Stephen Lawrence's story, because neither he, nor his parents, nor any one of us, would ever forgive silence.

Rationale

The context of this task is the topic of racism. It is a speech for my fellow students in an assembly. We studied texts in all four parts for this topic, and for part one we read political speeches, including Martin Luther King's *I have a dream,* President Obama's first acceptance speech and Nelson Mandela's speech at his trial before his imprisonment. We also learned about the murder of Stephen Lawrence through a variety of sources.

I was moved and shocked by the injustices and open racism of the police, and decided to write a speech about it to draw the attention of my fellow students to the long term injustice. I wanted to convey the incredible immorality of the situation, so I set my speech a decade after the murder, when it still did not look as if there would ever be any sort of justice for Stephen Lawrence's family.

I wanted to show the shock I felt and make my audience feel it too. I used stylistic features I had identified when analysing King's speech, and also in President Obama's first acceptance speech. Both of these use repetition of important points, as I do when I describe the "story" with different adjectives – this builds up the shocking effect. I also use repetition as part of my structure, repeating an idea at the beginning of different paragraphs, and returning to the beginning at the end, having explained the sense in which the case can seriously be called a story. We usually think of stories as being entertaining, and I try to show that they can be a good way to make social criticism as well. I include the audience by using the first person plural just as President Obama does.

300 words
Source references:
The Macpherson Report, 24th February 1999
The Colour of Justice – BBC documentary, 1999

Sample examiner comment

Criterion A: Rationale

The rationale successfully links the task to the course, identifying the influences from the different parts of the course that contributed to it. It shows how the choice of text type is integral to the purpose of the task; why the topic was engaging; how it develops the topic; and how language was used to convey meaning. The rationale addresses all the key assessment criteria. Reference to current developments of the investigation demonstrate a lively engagement with the issue.

Criterion B: Task and content

The task shows excellent understanding of and engagement with the topic. The content is consistently appropriate to the task – the selection of evidence makes the speech authentic and convincing. There is detailed knowledge and understanding of the topic, demonstrated in comment on the implications of police handling of events. The task shows excellent understanding of the power of the chosen text type to convey meaning.

Criterion C: Organisation

This task demonstrates the importance of careful planning – the structure is excellent, with the introduction being picked up in the conclusion. Clear understanding is demonstrated of the connection between literary and non-literary language, in the framework of the "story." The task illustrates the candidate's understanding of the potential of rhetorical devices to persuade. The text type is used convincingly and with sophistication. The task is very well organised. The structure is excellent.

Criterion D: Language

Language and style are clear and effective. Style is consistent with the task. Register is consistently appropriate. There are occasional grammatical errors.

Drafting a written task – some questions answered

Do I need a bibliography?

Not necessarily a full bibliography, but you need to include a list of references appropriate to your task.

Can I exceed the word count?

No; part of the task is to work within the framework of the word count.

Can my task relate to more than one part of the course?

It will probably relate to more than one part of the course; but you must be clear which part is your specific focus. If you are developing an idea that is media focused, your task will be part two related; if you are looking at rhetoric, or language change, or language reflecting prejudice, your task will be part one related. It is easier to see where tasks belong when they focus on one of your part three or part four literary works. You have to account on the cover sheet and in your rationale for which part of the course your task relates to.

Who decides on the subject of my task?

You do. This is your response to the course, and your work. You can ask your teacher for guidance when you select a topic, text type and task.

Is there any text type I can't choose?

You may not write an essay; otherwise, so long as you work within the word count, and demonstrate understanding of the conventions of the text type you have chosen, you can choose freely.

Can I use the same topic for my written task as for a further oral activity?

Yes. But the content must be different.

When should I do the written task?

You will do written tasks throughout the course and for every topic. It is likely that the one you submit for assessment will be done later in the course, when you have worked on all your topics. You have to complete three at standard level and four at higher, so you will clearly be devising written tasks throughout the course.

Who assesses the written task(s)?

These are externally assessed.

Can the written task be done collaboratively?

No. This has to be your own work.

Chapter Five

Introduction to Internal Assessment

The internally assessed part of the course has two elements; one of these, the Individual Oral Commentary (IOC) addresses the literary works you read in Part Four of the course, Literature – Critical Study. At standard level you will read two, and at higher level you will read three, and all will be selected from the Prescribed List of Authors.

The other element is the Further Oral Activities (FOAs,) which address part one and part two of the course. Each of these elements carries a maximum mark of 15%, so that the Internal Assessment part of the course contributes 30% of the overall total. Look back at the assessment section in Chapter One to see how this all fits together.

The marks for the assessed tasks arising from Part Four, then, is weighted equally between your oral response to literary and to non-literary texts. However the study for Part Four is literary, and it consists of the works you read for this part – two at standard level and three at higher level. These texts are the focus of the IOC. The other part of the oral assessment, the FOAs, takes place within your study of Parts One and Two. The assessment criteria are different for the two elements, to reflect the different focus of the tasks.

We will look at these two elements separately, but it will be useful to consider what is expected of you before we do that.

The internal Oral Commentary (IOC)

What is the focus of the IOC?

Part Four is the close study of literary texts. In Part Three you also read literary texts, but your focus is on the whole work. Even though you will be assessed on your response to the work as a whole, you do have to demonstrate some knowledge and understanding of how writers use language – you need to recognise grammatical, lexical and stylistic choices a writer makes in order to understand and explain how she or he conveys meaning. It is one of the aspects you take into consideration in your response to the examination question, along with theme and context.

In Part Four, on the other hand, the close focus is on looking at the detail of how a short extract of text is written, rather than looking more broadly at the whole work. This is called a *commentary,* and it is your competence in this aspect of reading literary texts that you will reflect in your IOC. The learning outcomes explain this.

What are the learning outcomes for Part Four (The IOC)?

There are three main areas to think about:

- You have to read your literary works in detail, so you can show your understanding of how writers convey their meaning, explicitly and implicitly; that is, what they choose not to say openly, but imply through the omission, as well as what they do say directly. In other words, the meaning does not have to be explained directly. You also have to be able to explain where in the whole work your extract comes from.

- You have to show your understanding of themes and how they indicate and illustrate such things as the writer's moral or ethical position in the work. You can show this by using evidence from the text that illustrates the writer's position, and by considering as well how point of view can be conveyed differently in different genres.

- You have to make clear your understanding of a relevant critical vocabulary. You will do this by using the terminology appropriate to your analysis, showing that you recognise and apply it accurately. (See the glossary) You will reflect this in, for instance, your discussion of characterisation; vocabulary, sentence structure and grammar; use of imagery; and other critical aspects of the work or extract.

How will I be assessed for the IOC?

The assessment criteria are the same for both levels, and assess all candidates on their ability to present an organised, coherent oral commentary on an extract of a literary work they have studied during the course. You are expected to use the appropriate critical vocabulary, and, except when reference to other parts of the work throws light on your commentary, to focus entirely on the extract itself.

The IOC is recorded, marked by your teachers, and moderated externally by an IB moderator. It is a formal procedure, so remember to reflect that in your language and approach – don't be conversational, even though you know your teacher well; this can lead to sloppy choices of vocabulary, and you need to show you have an adequate, appropriate critical range.

What are the assessment criteria?

There are four assessment criteria:

Criterion A assesses the extent to which your commentary shows that you know and understand your text well, and can support your comments with well chosen references to the text. You need o show that you understand the author's theme(s) or message, and that you are very familiar with the text.
Marks available: 10

Criterion B assesses the extent to which you understand the use and effect of literary features. You need to explain the effects of literary features (such as structure, style, use of imagery) and also show you understand the way the use of literary features adds to and is part of the meaning; in other words, identify the literary features and say how and why they are used.

Marks available: 10

Criterion C assesses the organisation and structure of your presentation; is it organised and coherent?
Marks available: 5

Criterion D assesses your use of language. Is your grammar correct? Is your vocabulary varied? Is your register appropriate, and not conversational? Do you use the necessary critical terms?
Marks available: 5

In total, 30 marks are available for the IOC.

How does Part Four differ from Part Three?

Part Three

There are more similarities than differences; the main difference is one of focus, and this shows in the different methods of assessment. For Part Three you have to address the bigger picture – that literature is part of our experience as human beings, a means of communicating about the problems, pains and joys of life however, wherever and whenever we live. And you have to do this in relation to close knowledge of the two or three (standard or higher) works you have read for your study. You take a written exam at the end of the course.

Part Four

For Part Four you have to attend to the minute detail of how the use of language in a text creates its meaning; and of what effect the choice of language and stylistic features has. You do this in relation to the close study of your two or three (standard or higher) Part Four works.

You take what is, to all intents and purposes, an oral exam at the end of the course, on a date decided by your school in line with IB internal assessment deadlines.

How do the literary works differ?

The different methods of assessment, taking into account the role or function of literary works on the one hand and the way they use language on the other, call for different aspects of texts, and this influences the works chosen. For Part Three the texts must be especially rich in ideas, while for Part Four they must be especially rich in language. This is because in paper 2 you will write about the ideas in the whole work, whereas in the IOC you will be looking exclusively at an extract of no more than forty lines from one work.

To distinguish between texts in this way is arbitrary, of course, and again reflects a focus rather than a difference. You will look at the stylistic features of any and all literary works, just as you will look in all of them at what the writer means – the themes. Most texts would be positioned equally well in either part, and all critical considerations apply to both assessments.

One consequence, though, is that you are much more likely to study poetry in Part Four than in Part Three. This is where it sits most comfortably, given its very particular, carefully worked, complex use of language and stylistic features. Its length lends itself readily to the IOC.

Considering poetry

Hopefully, you will have discovered on your path through life – and on this course in particular – that poetry is a fantastic way of expressing the essence of life's experiences – it is, in a way we sometimes find hard to explain, a way of sharing our humanity.

What you will certainly have seen during the course is that poetry conveys meaning just like any other genre or text type, and is born of the same imperative human need to communicate. Every topic you have studied for English A: Language and Literature will probably have included poetry, whether it is conflict, inequality, racism, climate change, education or anything else. Along with blogs, speeches, journalistic articles, research documents, film documentaries, television news programmes, plays, texts, novels, academic essays, short stories and countless other text types, poems communicate meaning. Like any other text type, they can make us laugh or cry; they can make us angry or confused; they can shock or entertain; they can teach us and help us to understand; they can celebrate or commemorate; poems are a means of expression, and like other text types they have their own characteristic ways of using language. They do not have a language of their own, with different vocabulary and stylistic features – poetry is not a "foreign" language. Rhythm, rhyme, imagery, exaggeration, pathos, onomatopoeia, alliteration, – these and other terms that tend to be associated particularly with poetry are to be found in everyday life; in our conversations, lessons, television programmes, advertisements, newspapers. While there is no different language for poetry, however, there is distinctive use of it, and this is what we mean when we talk about poetic conventions.

The consideration of poetry as a genre or text type falls naturally in Part Four of the course. The thorough and detailed approach to the analysis of language in poetry is comparable with the approach you need to develop for the analysis not only of other literary texts, but of non-literary texts as well. Learning how to comment on a poem will help you to comment effectively on an advertisement, for instance; even though the advertisement is likely to lean towards persuasive language, and the poem towards imagery. It is useful to remember this, since you can expect any text type or genre in paper one, including poetry.

Analysis and "the language of poetry"

Poetry is usually instantly recognisable because of the way it appears on the page, and because very often when we read it the language seems "heightened" – full of imagery, suggesting or implying rather than stating openly, using language in a complex way not often found in other genres or text types. For some people this makes it inaccessible; for many people it makes poetry seem difficult. Given a choice, they would avoid analysing a poem. If you think about it in much the same way as you would think about analysing an advertisement, however, it will feel less separate from other text types.

You have to "read" an advertisement – that is, take into account verbal and graphic aspects as well as thinking about context, audience and purpose and the way they affect meaning. With poetry, you look at form – this is sometimes referred to as structure - as well as the ways language is used, in conjunction with purpose and context, to see how the poet conveys meaning. Audience is often less of a consideration when you analyse poetry, and you may well find that you don't need to comment on it because it seems obvious: there is nothing analytical about saying that the poem is written for people who read poetry; stating the obvious is not critical comment. So, just as there are considerations you have to address when you analyse persuasive texts, there are features of poetry you have to think about when you analyse a poem. Those features are explained here, and you will also find the terms used in the glossary.

What is form?

This is the structure of poetry. It has several aspects; it includes what you see as well as what you hear: shape – the way the poem looks on the page; and sound – the musical effect of metre, rhythm and rhyme. These play a fundamental part in conveying the meaning of poetry.

Poems can be written in any form the poet chooses, and these choices are not randomly made – they are planned very carefully so that the form of the poem contributes in the most effective way to the meaning the poet wants to convey. The length of the lines, the length of the poem, the number and arrangement of the stanzas, the metrical pattern – all of these contribute to form.

Some forms have been around for centuries and some have been developed more recently; like all literature, and like language itself, poetry is a living entity that changes with people and through time. Poets develop their own ways of speaking relevantly to their time and context, building on the work of their predecessors and peers.

Ballad form

The ballad is a good example of this; it is possibly the earliest form of verse in the European tradition. Travelling musicians would go from village to village to sing songs, the lyrics of which were the ballad, telling stories of great victories or defeats in battles, or of broken hearted lovers who have been abandoned – stories we think of as traditional folk tales – and, because most people, including the musician, did not read, the stories used very strong rhythm and rhyme as a way to remember what came next. We can say that the ballad is a useful poetic form for telling stories. Its simplicity led poets to develop it much later, in the nineteenth and twentieth centuries, as an effective means of conveying satire; in the second half of the twentieth century the ballad was given a broad audience and renewed popularity as a form when it was used to express protest against evils confronting society like war, the proliferation of nuclear weapons, racism and other major social and political issues.

The ballad is a simple form, and over time poets developed more complex forms capable of carrying subtle, complex ideas. These reflections on the nature of the ballad show how important it would be in a commentary to address context, since it is relevant to audience and purpose as well as to theme.

The sonnet

The sonnet is a very tightly organised form, fourteen lines long, with a set rhyme scheme and a rhyming couplet at the end. Sonnets don't tell heroic tales – the form is not appropriate – but they often reflect on one idea in different ways. The final rhyming couplet comments on the idea that has been developed in the preceding twelve lines. The first twelve lines are organised formally, usually either in three groups of four lines – each group of four is called a quatrain; or one group of eight lines – an octave – and one group of six lines – a sestet. (If you have studied sonnets in Part Four you will be familiar with these terms, and if you haven't you won't need them, so don't panic about the apparent huge injection of technical terms.) Each of these groups has its own rhyme scheme. The development of ideas in the sonnet tends to follow the grouping of the lines; whatever the arrangement of lines, the rhyming couplet at the end comments in some way on their meaning.

Irregular form

The sonnet and the ballad are probably the most widely known examples of regular forms, where the form is the frame within which the poet writes. In your commentary you would reflect on this *regular* form. Not all poems have regular form, however, and so there may be no rhythm or rhyme scheme to comment on, or regular pattern of lines and stanzas. You would call this *irregular* form. Like many developments of already existing forms, the use of irregular form was developed in the twentieth century. Poets started to ask questions about the nature of poetry: is it simply its form? If you take away the form is it still poetry? Or is poetry a way of seeing the world? Who is poetry for – does it have to be only for an educated elite audience? What should poetry concern itself with? Are there some subjects that are poetic in nature? These and many other such fundamental questions influenced developments in poetic form, resulting in a much freer use of it.

Many poets use adaptations of existing forms. You might find, for instance, that a poem has two lines that rhyme in every eight; or that one line in five is rhythmical; when you read such a poem, you have to work out why – does it highlight the message? Is it a factor in the form of the poem? What does it contribute to the poem's meaning?

These developments occurred in response to some of the problems that can arise in absolutely regular poems; a poet following a rigid rhyme scheme, for instance, might have to choose words that were inappropriate, possibly preventing the poem from being serious. Strict patterns of rhythm can make a poem sound superficial or silly. It is considerations like these that make poets experiment with form, seeing how far it can be adapted.

"Shape" as form

Other poetic forms show similarly that form influences the way language is used. In "shape" poetry; some poets have exploited the visual aspect of poetry to make their poems look like the object they describe – a snail, for instance, or a flock of birds. This approach to poetry became popular in the twentieth century, but four hundred years earlier George Herbert, a contemporary of Shakespeare, had written a poem about the spiritual mysteries of the Christian Easter. He called it *Easter Wings,* and arranged the lines in the two stanzas of the poem so they looked like two pairs of wings. The idea that the appearance on the page of a poem can contribute to its meaning is not new.

Other poets use shape to enhance or underline their meaning.

One example of this is Louis MacNeice's poem *Prayer Before Birth,* which appears later in this section, with notes commenting on it.

Some technical terms related to form

Form is critically important, then. What follows is a description of some of the key critical terms you will need to be able to discuss it.

Rhyme

This refers to one of the sound effects of poetry. We hear it. We most often think of it as occurring at the end of lines in a poem. It helps us to remember what comes next. It can be comic.

On the other hand, it can have the most powerful effect when it occurs not at the end of a line, but in the middle of it, as for example in Louis Macneice's poem *Prayer Before Birth:*

Let not the bloodsucking bat or the rat or the stoat or the
Club-footed ghoul come near me

There are many different sorts of rhyme, both at the end of lines – end rhyme – and in the middle of a line – internal rhyme. They are all part of the poem's structure, and chosen by the poet to contribute to the meaning in some way. The glossary includes explanations of the various sorts of rhyme you might need to address in your IOC and in Paper One.

Rhythm and metre

Rhythm is another aspect of form that you hear. So far we have not discussed *metre,* but the two terms are very closely connected. Metre is the musical pattern created by the regular stresses in a poem. Metre is the beat of a poem, to put it very simply. It can make the poem seem sad or happy, urgent or relaxed, serious or light-hearted – it really can create the mood. Although metre is rhythmical, rhythm is not just another word for metre; rhythm also refers to patterns of language – so when we say that the use of enjambement and caesura creates the rhythm of speech in a poem, we mean it enables the poet to use the *natural* sound of speech; form in poetry is contrived rather than natural, like any art form, and metre is one of the elements that contribute to it.

Stanza or verse

A stanza is a visible section of a poem, made up of a few lines; explanations often liken a stanza in poetry to a paragraph in prose. The stanza is a fundamental aspect of form. In some poems the stanzas are all the same length – four lines, for example – while in others the stanzas are all different lengths. You will need to explain what effect this has on the meaning of the poem.

The words *stanza* and *verse* mean the same thing, and you will come across them both in your background reading. *Stanza* is slightly more useful because it is the only word in the English language for the sections of a poem, whereas the word *verse* also refers to the whole of a literary genre. You could say, "I like verse more than I like prose" to indicate your preference for poetry over the novel, for instance. Neither is wrong, however, and you may use either or both.

Enjambement and caesura

Many poets would say that the effect of working within a regular form gives their use of language an intensity and depth that they cannot achieve otherwise. They therefore want to keep the form, but avoid its limitations. One device they use to do this is called *enjambement* – when the meaning does not stop at the end of every line. It carries on until the sentence or phrase is finished, thus giving the poem the rhythm of speech. Another device, very closely connected with it, is called *caesura*. This is a break in the middle of a line, and it also helps to create the rhythm of speech. These two devices make a poem sound more natural, while the poem may be written in very regular form.

For example:

> *I am not yet born; provide me*
> *With water to dandle me, grass to grow for me,*

Diction

Diction is the poet's choice of words in a poem. It isn't really an aspect of form, but it is important because the choice of words creates mood, atmosphere and tone. It is the poet's diction that makes the poem sound angry or cheerful, happy or sad, upbeat or downbeat, formal or informal. When you are addressing rhythm and rhyme, the poet's choice of words may well be something you want to include.

All of these critical elements are aspects of form, and if you have to comment on a poem in your IOC you will need to refer to them. If there is a poem in Paper One, you will also refer to them.

What will the IOC look like?

The IOC consists of an extract of up to forty lines from one of your Part Four works, with two guiding questions. One of these questions will focus on the content of the extract – what is going on in this extract relating to narrative, theme, context and so on; the other question will focus on some aspect of how language is used in the extract. You will be given the extract with the questions at the beginning of your twenty minutes' supervised preparation time. Your IOC will take place at the end of this time.

The IOC will be recorded; it will consist of a presentation by you on your extract that lasts for about ten minutes; in the remaining five minutes your teacher will lead a discussion with you about your presentation and any points you may need to develop. The point of this is not to catch you out – it is to ensure that you demonstrate completely your understanding of the details of the extract and its significance within the whole work.

What follows is a sample IOC text; the poem is annotated in preparation for the presentation on page 92. The questions will be specific to your extract or poem, neither about the whole text nor general. They will not be numbered. This is what your extract will look like:

Individual Oral Commentary

I am not yet born; O hear me.
Let not the bloodsucking bat or the rat or the stoat or the
    club-footed ghoul come near me.

I am not yet born, console me.
I fear that the human race may with tall walls wall me,
    with strong drugs dope me, with wise lies lure me,
      on black racks rack me, in blood-baths roll me.

I am not yet born; provide me
With water to dandle me, grass to grow for me, trees to talk
    to me, sky to sing to me, birds and a white light
      in the back of my mind to guide me.

I am not yet born; forgive me
For the sins that in me the world shall commit, my words
    when they speak me, my thoughts when they think me,
      my treason engendered by traitors beyond me,
        my life when they murder by means of my
          hands, my death when they live me.

I am not yet born; rehearse me
In the parts I must play and the cues I must take when
    old men lecture me, bureaucrats hector me, mountains
      frown at me, lovers laugh at me, the white
        waves call me to folly and the desert calls
          me to doom and the beggar refuses
            my gift and my children curse me.

I am not yet born; O hear me,
Let not the man who is beast or who thinks he is God come near
    me.

I am not yet born; O fill me
With strength against those who would freeze my
    humanity, would dragoon me into a lethal automaton,
      would make me a cog in a machine, a thing with
        one face, a thing, and against all those who
          would dissipate my entirety, would
            blow me like thistledown hither
              and thither or hither and thither
                like water held in the
                  hands would spill me.

Let them not make me a stone and let them not spill me.
Otherwise kill me.

Louis MacNeice

Guiding questions:

- What features of society does MacNeice identify and condemn?
- How does MacNeice use poetic devices to convey his feelings about society?

How can I prepare for my IOC?

The steps to being prepared are basic:

- Know your Part Four works really well. There should be no need to say here again that one reading is not enough – you need to read exam texts several times and be thoroughly familiar with them.

- Make sure that you have learned the critical vocabulary you need to discuss the extract in detail. You will have been keeping a list of terms as you have come across them during the course, with illustrating examples from your own texts – this will prove invaluable.

- Read through the glossary – it will help you to revise what you know.

- Practise by choosing samples from your works and analysing them.
  One useful exercise for this type of assessment is to identify key moments in a work; think about critical episodes in the narrative, or moments of revelation about a character, or turning points in the development of a tragedy, places where the theme is particularly clearly addressed, passages where the use of language is most noticeable. Find them in the work, and count forty lines around them – very often such moments fit into forty or so lines of text – they wouldn't be key moments if they last for many pages. These passages will provide you with excellent practice material. You should go through them very carefully, linking them to the whole text, identifying stylistic features and so on. You could well get such a passage in your IOC.

- Familiarise yourself with the assessment criteria.

- Check that you understand the learning outcomes.

Preparing the commentary – working on the extract

In your twenty minutes' preparation time, you will have to go through your extract identifying everything that needs comment, and indicating what that is. You won't know in advance which of your Part Four works your extract will come from, but you know all of them so there won't be any unpleasant surprises. This time is therefore useful to plan a coherent response to an extract from a work you know; to organise your ideas in the light of the specific questions. The list below suggests a way of approaching the preparation time. It does this by including questions you should/could ask yourself as well as giving some *"Dos and Don'ts"*. The list is obviously not exhaustive – it couldn't be, when you will have a particular forty line extract to comment on and this is general guidance. It is simply an attempt to show you that if you get all your ideas down on to the extract, you will quite quickly be able to group them together logically.

Annotating the extract

➤ Go through it carefully – write all over it. This is the best way to ensure that your commentary is specific and detailed.

➤ Underline or highlight words or phrases.

➤ Identify all the stylistic, grammatical, poetic, literary, dramatic features you can find. Think about form if it is drama or especially if it is a poem. Identify characteristics of its genre.

➤ Jot down links between the extract and the whole – does it exemplify particular use of stylistic features? Does it illustrate the theme particularly well? Is its place in the narrative especially significant? When you have done this, you will be able to see which comments go together to make your answer coherent.

➤ Avoid going through the extract line by line in your presentation. You will go through it line by line as you prepare, but only so that you collect all the points you need to deliver a coherent presentation.

➤ While you don't have to consider the guiding questions one after the other, you do have to make sure that your answer addresses them, and it is sensible to think of referring your commentary to them in your conclusion. Show that you recognise the need to talk about language as well as theme.

➤ In your planning, even in the introduction, do not summarise the narrative or retell the story; be aware of this particularly if your extract is from a play, novel or short story.

➤ Make sure you have an introductory sentence, possibly identifying the work and contextualising the extract in the whole if it comes from a longer work. If it is a poem, you could give an overview of the main theme. Keep the introduction short and very clear.

Example of an annotated sample from an IOC

The following example of an annotated poem in preparation for the IOC gets as near as possible to presenting it as the candidate did. It shows how the annotations lead to an organised response to the questions. It is unlikely that you have read *Prayer Before Birth* for Part Four, so this plan serves as a suggested approach rather than as revision.

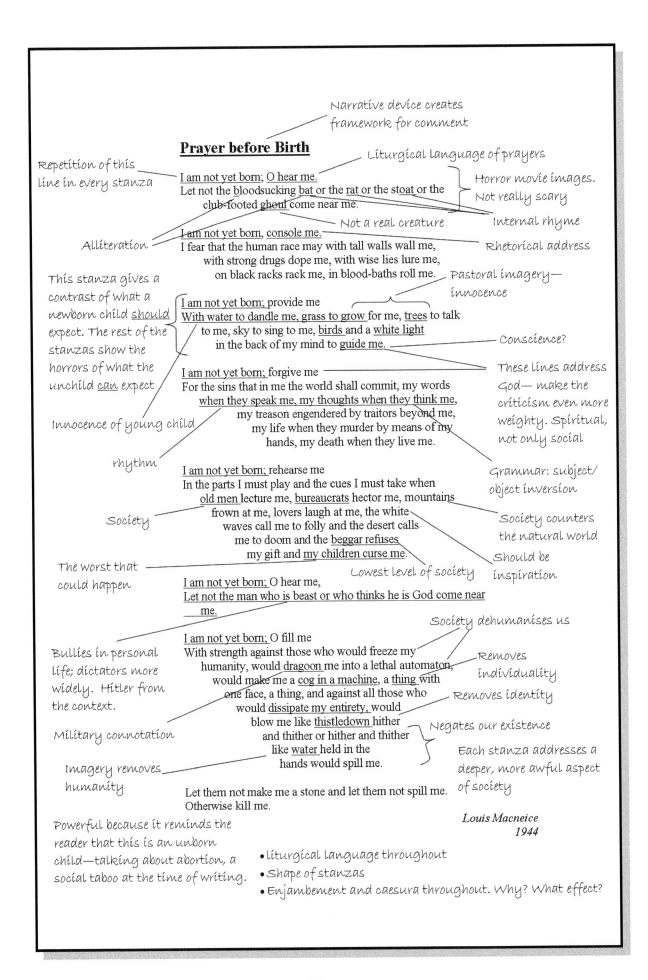

Prayer before Birth

Narrative device creates framework for comment

Liturgical language of prayers

Repetition of this line in every stanza

I am not yet born; O hear me.
Let not the bloodsucking bat or the rat or the stoat or the
club-footed ghoul come near me.

Horror movie images. Not really scary

Not a real creature

Internal rhyme

I am not yet born, console me.
I fear that the human race may with tall walls wall me,
with strong drugs dope me, with wise lies lure me,
on black racks rack me, in blood-baths roll me.

Alliteration

Rhetorical address

This stanza gives a contrast of what a newborn child should expect. The rest of the stanzas show the horrors of what the unchild can expect

I am not yet born; provide me
With water to dandle me, grass to grow for me, trees to talk
to me, sky to sing to me, birds and a white light
in the back of my mind to guide me.

Pastoral imagery— innocence

Conscience?

Innocence of young child

I am not yet born; forgive me
For the sins that in me the world shall commit, my words
when they speak me, my thoughts when they think me,
my treason engendered by traitors beyond me,
my life when they murder by means of my
hands, my death when they live me.

These lines address God— make the criticism even more weighty. Spiritual, not only social

rhythm

I am not yet born; rehearse me
In the parts I must play and the cues I must take when
old men lecture me, bureaucrats hector me, mountains
frown at me, lovers laugh at me, the white
waves call me to folly and the desert calls
me to doom and the beggar refuses
my gift and my children curse me.

Grammar: subject/ object inversion

Society counters the natural world

Society

Should be inspiration

The worst that could happen

I am not yet born; O hear me,
Let not the man who is beast or who thinks he is God come near
me.

Lowest level of society

Society dehumanises us

Bullies in personal life; dictators more widely. Hitler from the context.

I am not yet born; O fill me
With strength against those who would freeze my
humanity, would dragoon me into a lethal automaton,
would make me a cog in a machine, a thing with
one face, a thing, and against all those who
would dissipate my entirety, would
blow me like thistledown hither
and thither or hither and thither
like water held in the
hands would spill me.

Removes individuality

Removes identity

Military connotation

Negates our existence

Imagery removes humanity

Each stanza addresses a deeper, more awful aspect of society

Let them not make me a stone and let them not spill me.
Otherwise kill me.

Louis Macneice
1944

Powerful because it reminds the reader that this is an unborn child—talking about abortion, a social taboo at the time of writing.

• liturgical language throughout
• Shape of stanzas
• Enjambement and caesura throughout. Why? What effect?

92

Sample plan

The next step is to put all of these points into a sequence that is coherent. The following plan, based entirely on the annotations above, is one way of doing this. It leaves plenty of room to add references to the poem, and to add to the introduction and conclusion. Remember, though, that there is no one optimum plan, and that how you organise your ideas will depend very greatly on the extract you are commenting on. Your plan will be in note form – you are writing only enough to organise your ideas into a coherent order.

Introduction

- Theme – very strong criticism of society that depersonalises, dehumanises and destroys people.
- Language – use of sound effects in poetry makes his anger seem very strong.

Main body

Points to include:
- Theme – poet's message about society
- Comprehensive list of all aspects and the damage they do
- Gets more subtle as it goes
- Society abuses the innocent
- Shocks with the idea of killing an unborn child – extreme, so it underlines his anger and horror; even though now abortions are regular events, they are still something of a taboo
- Criticises individuals and institutions and the whole of society

Language

- The narrative voice is that of an unborn child – idea of innocence and abuse see stanza 3 imagery
- Chronology of abuse goes from horror movie type (ghouls, stanza 1) to historical (stanza 2) that we don't take too seriously to "cog in a machine" stanza 7 that we can empathise with. Does this with imagery (quote)
- Uses rhetorical language (O hear me) to give it the sense of prayer – deepens the outrage; spiritual as well as social/emotional
- Leads to destroying the human spirit – stanza 7
- Stanza 8 the ultimate horror

Other poetic features

- Imagery – e.g. similes and metaphors stanza 7 – like thistledown; make me a cog in a machine
- Allusion to Hitler stanza 6 – the context of the date makes this clear
- Enjambement and caesura all stanzas – quote 7
- Inversion of subject and object to make the reader think – stanza 4
- Form – the shape echoing the intensity of the meaning – the visual whole
- These work with tone – anger; the repetition, pace, contrast between quick and slow parts.
- Impact on reader – shock of abortion as solution/(especially in context of time of writing) Fear.

Conclusion

In this poem MacNeice says that society is entirely destructive of the human identity and soul. He uses many poetic devices to make his message effective and memorable, and shocks the reader into hearing what he has to say.

You can see from this example that one person's plan would not necessarily help another – you have to write your own. What it does show is that you can organise your ideas into a logical sequence, and identify the quotations you want to use, by annotating in detail. This plan would take you through your IOC satisfactorily. It addresses both the questions, is organised, quotes from and refers to the extract, and is specific throughout.

Final comments

- Some people find the prospect of the IOC scary; but you know your works and have learned the critical vocabulary – you are in control, and don't need to be apprehensive.

- The IOC is a close analysis of an extract of literary writing. Whichever work it comes from, you must keep in mind that it is the extract you are analysing, and not the entire work.

- Only refer to the whole work if it is necessary for your commentary on the forty lines you have been given.

- Your task is to comment on *what* is said in your extract, and on *how* it is said. That is, on *content* and *language*. The guiding questions will reflect this.

- Don't give a potted biography of the author, or list other works. This is sometimes a feature of introductions – it is unnecessary. Doing this loses marks because it is irrelevant and unfocused.

- Plan your presentation. You have learned in every part of the course that planning is important – don't forget that now. Make notes during the preparation time. Write all over your copy of the extract – that is one way of ensuring that you comment from the text and don't become general.

- Quote from the extract in your presentation; doing so will ensure that you stay focused.

- Make sure you have a clear introductory sentence, and a clear concluding sentence. With these, even if the main body of your presentation isn't entirely well organised, you will gain marks in criterion C because you are thinking about structure.

- Familiarise yourself with the assessment criteria; they will help to keep you on track.

- Remember that your teacher is there to ensure that your performance is as good as it can be. If you are unclear, or if you omit something important, your teacher's questions will help you to clarify or complete your commentary.

The Further Oral Activities (FOAs)

Introduction to the FOAs

The FOAs are the mechanism by which you are assessed orally on Part One and Part Two of the course; you are assessed on at least one activity from each part. The activities are based on texts arising from the study of your topics in Parts One and Two, and are worth15% of the overall total. This means that the mark allocation for your oral assessments is equally distributed between literary and non-literary texts.

By the time you are preparing for your final exams, you will have completed all your FOAs, but it is useful to see what they assess, how they are assessed, how they fit in with the rest of the course, and what they consist of.

What do the FOAs assess?

You will have read texts of many different types during the course. All of them fit in the context of your topics. The non-literary text types are the particular focus of Part One and Part Two. Part One addresses the relationship between language and cultural context; Part Two addresses the relationship between language and mass communication. The topics you have studied have enabled you to explore the connections between texts, their contexts (cultural, historical, social), the language they use and their meaning.

It is your knowledge and understanding of this that the FOAs assess. They require you to demonstrate your understanding of how language creates meaning, in the various different ways it is used, for different purposes, at different times and in different cultural contexts. This is outlined in Chapter Two, in the section that gives an overview of the course content; the learning outcomes for each part of the course are described, and those for Parts One and Two are the ones addressed by the FOAs.

What sort of activity is suitable for an FOA?

The purpose of the FOA is to enable you to demonstrate the rather conceptual learning outcomes of Part One and Part Two in a creative way. There are many possibilities; they can be group or individual activities. It must be clear with each task that there is a close link with texts you have studied in the relevant part of the course: Part One – Language in cultural context or Part Two – Language and mass communication. Your activities arise from these texts, or are inspired by them. Unlike the IOC, the FOAs are not the close analysis of individual short texts. The possible activities include any of the following:

- Structured group discussion of various sorts, led by the student(s) being assessed. For example, a class discussion, based on a text about the language of prejudice

- Role play – a dialogue or interview, perhaps, focusing on changes in language, or how the media use language to persuade

- Dramatic presentation – creating a short play or scene exploring an issue raised in a text from one of your topics

96

- Individual oral presentation – you could give a formal speech on one of your topics, comment on a specific text, look at the interface between image and word... In fact, you may present a considered oral response to any text(s) or aspect of text(s) you find particularly interesting or challenging.

This list makes some suggestions; there are many more ways you could demonstrate orally your understanding of the concepts underpinning Parts One and Two.

When you start planning your activity you need to look back at the learning outcomes for the relevant part – One or Two – and show understanding of one or more of them through your response to the texts you have chosen. You need to know what it is about language that you want to reflect on through your activity before you start planning it. These are your aims. When you finish your activity you have to write a reflective statement commenting on your activity and how you achieved your aims, so you need to know from the outset what your aims and objectives are.

How will I be assessed?

The FOAs are worth 15% of the overall total score. Assessment of the FOAs is done by your teacher. They are not recorded, but a description of the activity and the marks awarded to the better of your two compulsory activities are sent to the IB external moderator along with the recording and marks of your IOC. You are marked according to the assessment criteria for the FOA.

The assessment criteria

There are four criteria:

Criterion A: Knowledge and understanding of the text(s) and subject matter or extract

You need to show that you know about the subject you have chosen as the focus of your activity, and that you understand the text you are addressing. You need to show how the subject and the text relate to each other. To what extent do you do this?
Marks available: 10

Criterion B: Understanding of how language is used
Your activity needs to show that you understand how the language used creates meaning, and how features of style and language are used especially effectively in your text. To what extent do you do this?
Marks available: 10

Criterion C: Organisation
Your activity needs to be well organised and coherently structured. To what extent are you successful in doing so?
Marks available: 5

Criterion D: Language:
You need to use accurate, varied and clear language, and appropriate register and style. To what extent do you do so?
Marks available: 5

How do the FOAs relate to the rest of the course?

- They are based on the content of Part One and Part Two of the course. Your activities are developments or explorations of texts from those two parts.

- They develop the analytical skills you need for paper one; they require you to consider interconnection between written and visual aspects of texts. This helps preparation for paper one.

- They help you to understand the significance of context, purpose and audience and their impact on language use. This helps preparation for paper one.

- They help you to understand choices of register, tone, language features, imagery, and other stylistic features in non-literary texts; you can then apply this understanding to literary texts. This helps your preparation for both paper one and the IOC.

- They help you to understand the significance of context on the way meaning is conveyed in a text. This will help you with paper two.

- The list above includes specific ways that the further oral activities contribute to or integrate with the other parts of the course. They also work together in the way all the separate parts do to develop your understanding of how context, purpose and audience influence the way language is used to convey meaning.

Final thoughts

Even though you will have completed your FOAs by the time you start your serious exam preparation, it is worth thinking about the ways they require you to interact with language yourself; for your activities you reflected on how other people use language and are influenced by their purpose, who they are addressing, when and where and in what circumstances they are writing. In addition you were the creator of your text, so you know that context, purpose and audience have an enormous influence on the way texts are constructed, and on how language is used to convey meaning. What you have learned while working for your FOAs has a valuable contribution to make to your remaining assessments.

Glossary

Useful terms for critical analysis

allegory
a narrative that has two separate meanings
example: The Crucible, by Arthur Miller, is allegorical in telling the story of the Salem witch hunts while referring to McCarthyism in 1950s USA

alliteration
where two or more words begin with the same sound and occur in sequence
example: 'the tingle tongue taste of Gibbs SR' in a 1950s toothpaste advertisement

allusion
a reference to something completely separate from the text in which it appears
example: MacNeice alludes to Hitler in his poem *Prayer Before Birth*: 'Let not the man who is beast or who thinks he is God come near me'

ambiguity
when a word or phrase has a double meaning

ambivalence
having mixed feelings about something
example: respecting the bravery of a soldier while believing that war is wrong

analogy
illustrating the subject under discussion by making a parallel comparison

analysis
the detailed study and explanation of a text

anecdote
the recounting of a small incident to illustrate a point; sometimes humorous

anthropomorphism
talking or writing about animals as though they were human beings
example: the animals in George Orwell's novel, *Animal Farm*

aphorism
the expression of a widely recognised truth about life in a standard form
example: 'red sky at night, shepherd's delight'

appeal
an appeal is a text, usually part of a campaign, most often aiming to fundraise

association of ideas
when one idea calls to mind another, often used in advertising

assonance
where two or more similar vowel sounds within words occur in sequence
example: 'with w<u>i</u>se l<u>ie</u>s lure me' (Prayer Before Birth by Louis MacNeice)

atmosphere	a general way of describing mood *example:* in films, music is often used to create atmosphere
ballad	a long, narrative poem characterised by regularity of rhythm and rhyme
bathos	comic shift from something important to something unimportant *example:* 'I got a box of chocolates for my birthday. The tragedy is, I don't like chocolate!'
bias	promoting one, specific, point of view in a text and deliberately excluding others
cacophony	unpleasant, inharmonious sound effect
caesura	a pause or break in the middle of a line of verse
campaign	a series or collection of different text types with one specific aim, frequently used in fundraising and in advertising
caption	brief text accompanying and explaining an image
caricature	an exaggerated depiction of a person
catharsis	the effect on the audience of the downfall of the tragic hero/ine; a feeling of relief or pity
characterisation	the way a writer creates a character in order to convince the reader
colloquial	informal language; often specific to particular social, local, or age-related groups
comedy	a broad literary genre which ends happily or satisfactorily
comic exaggeration	exaggeration for humorous effect
commentary	close, detailed description of a literary or non-literary text. This can be either written or oral and in both cases is structured as an essay.
connotation	the connotations of a word are its secondary meanings, overtones and implications
consonance	the repetition of consonant sounds at the end of a word, often found in poetry and in advertisements *example:* flip-flop
conventions	The particular aspects of language use that typify a text type are called its language conventions. They are the aspects of language use you would expect to find in a given text type. *example:* persuasive devices in an advertisement
critique	a reasoned criticism of a piece of writing
dialogue	a conversation between two people
diction	choice of vocabulary and phrases; for instance, can be conversational, rhetorical, formal or informal
dissonance	organisation of words that is not harmonious but discordant

dramatic irony	occurs in plays when the audience knows more about the events than the characters do, and so can understand the implications of the characters' thoughts and actions while the characters cannot
editorial	the article in a newspaper or journal which expresses the publication's opinions on the news
elegy	a formal literary tribute to someone who has died
emotive	creating emotion in the reader; not simply describing emotion
end rhyme	where rhyme occurs at the end of lines of verse

enjambement	where one line of poetry runs into the next, following the meaning, rather than stopping automatically at the end of the line
	example from Prayer Before Birth by Louis MacNeice:
	'I am not yet born; O fill me
	    With strength against those who would freeze my
	        humanity'

eye rhyme	where words look the same but sound different
fable	a story with a moral, intending to teach a lesson. George Orwell called *Animal Farm* a fable.
figurative language	language that is not literal
form	in poetry, usually the arrangement of lines and stanzas
genre	the word used to describe a literary text type
homonym	a word with more than one meaning, often used in puns *example: lead* can describe a heavy metal and an object used be for walking dogs
homophone	a word that sounds the same as another word but is spelled differently *example: mussel* and *muscle*
hyperbole	an extreme exaggeration *example:* to say, 'I'm starving,' when you are only slightly hungry
iambic metre	a rhythmical pattern of two syllables with emphasis on the second. One unit of iambic metre is called a foot.
iambic pentameter	five iambic feet
imagery	words that create a picture in the reader's mind, to make the thing being described clearer or more vivid
internal rhyme	where rhyme appears in the middle of lines *example:* 'Old men lecture me, bureaucrats hector me,' (Prayer Before Birth by Louis MacNeice)
interpretation	an understanding of the meaning of a text
irony	saying one thing and meaning another

layout	the way a text is presented on a page (applies to media, rather than literary, texts)
lexical set	repeated reference to one kind of imagery to create an overall effect
lexis	Vocabulary
liturgical	language typical of prayer and religion
lyrics	the words of a song
lyrical	with song-like effect
metaphor	a comparison in which the thing being described is said to be something else to make the description more vivid
metre	rhythm or beat
monologue	a piece of writing which is meant to be spoken by one person
mood	the feeling that is created in a text
motif	a recurring idea or image in a text
narrative	Story
narrative verse	poetry that tells a story
narrative voice	the point of view in which the plot is narrated
narrator	the person who tells the story
onomatopoeia	where a word sounds like the sound it is describing
oxymoron	a description of something which appears to be its opposite, or impossible *example:* an open secret
paradox	a statement which seems to be self-contradictory but upon reflection is logical *example:* from the Bob Dylan song, *Love Minus Zero/No Limit*, 'She knows there's no success like failure…'
parody	an imitation of a person intending to ridicule them
pastoral	describing a rural scene in an idealised, simple way; attributing idyllic qualities to the countryside and innocence to those who live there
pathos	when a great feeling of pity is created in a visual or written text
personification	giving human characteristics to something which is not human *example:* the sunlight danced on the rippling water
persuasive language	language used to encourage the reader to think or act in a particular way
plot	the plan and development of a narrative
protagonist	the main character in a literary work
pun	a play on words
quatrain	a four-line stanza

rationale	a reasoned explanation of a text
refrain	a repeated section, usually in poetry
repetition	saying or writing something more than once for a specific effect
rhetoric	the conventions of speaking for an audience
rhyme	the repetition of similar or identical sounds at the end of, or within, lines of poetry
rhyme scheme	the pattern of rhyme in a poem, usually at the end of the lines
rhyming couplet	a pair of consecutive lines in a poem which rhyme with each other. Sonnets end with a rhyming couplet
rhythm	a pattern of strong and weak beats
satire	the ridicule of something the writer dislikes
sensationalise	describing something in a exaggerated way to shock and engage the reader, frequently a characteristic of journalistic writing
setting	where and when the events of a story, play, or poem, take place
simile	a comparison in which the thing being described is said to be like another in order to make it more vivid *example:* describing someone feeling unwell as 'as white as a sheet'
soliloquy	a dramatic convention in which one person, alone on the stage, speaks their thoughts aloud
sonnet	a poem with fourteen lines, ending with a rhyming couplet
stanza	the grouping of lines in a poem; an individual verse in a poem
stereotype	the attribution of certain characteristics to a specific group of people, often the product of prejudiced ideas
stress	rhythmical emphasis (in poetry)
structure	the organising and ordering of ideas so that they are effective
style	the features that characterise a work, text type, publication or writer
syllable	one of the sections of sound that a word can be divided into, relevant in metre and rhyme *example:* au-to-ma-ton
symbol	an image that is used recurrently to represent a particular meaning in the text
syntax	choice and organisation of words in sentences
tautology	saying the same thing twice in different words, unnecessarily *example:* 'myself, I personally think…'

text	any verbal or visual production conveying meaning (note: this meaning is particular to IB English A: Language and Literature)
text type	the term used to describe a non-literary text
theme	the underlying meaning or idea in a text
tone	the character of a piece of writing, given to it by the voice of the narrator
tragedy	a technical term applied to drama, but which more broadly applies to other literary forms. In drama, a play in which the main character makes a mistake, realises their mistake and pays for it, usually with death.
vernacular	the language of a local context
verse	this can be either one stanza in a poem; or it can refer to the entirety of poetry. You might say: '… in the third verse of the poem…' or 'verse is my favourite literary genre'.
work	a literary text (note: this meaning is particular to IB English A: Language and Literature)

Appendices

Text 2

The British

Serves 60 million

Take some Picts, Celts and Silures
And let them settle,
Then overrun them with Roman conquerors.

Remove the Romans after approximately 400 years
Add lots of Norman French to some
Angles, Saxons, Jutes and Vikings, then stir vigorously.

Mix some hot Chileans, cool Jamaicans, Dominicans,
Trinidadians and Bajans with some Ethiopians, Chinese,
Vietnamese and Sudanese.

Then take a blend of Somalians, Sri Lankans, Nigerians
And Pakistanis,
Combine with some Guyanese
And turn up the heat.

Sprinkle some fresh Indians, Malaysians, Bosnians,
Iraqis and Bangladeshis together with some
Afghans, Spanish, Turkish, Kurdish, Japanese
And Palestinians
Then add to the melting pot.

Leave the ingredients to simmer.

As they mix and blend allow their languages to flourish
Binding them together with English.

Allow time to be cool.

Add some unity, understanding, and respect for the future,
Serve with justice
And enjoy.

Note: All the ingredients are equally important. Treating one ingredient better than
another will leave a bitter unpleasant taste.

Warning: An unequal spread of justice will damage the people and cause pain.

Give justice and equality to all.

Benjamin Zephaniah

Analyse, compare and contrast the following two texts. Include comments on the similarities and differences between the two texts and the significance of context, purpose, and formal and stylistic features.

Text 3

Charity condemns tourists' use of fresh water in developing countries

Study finds visitors to Bali, the Gambia and Goa use 16 times as much water as locals, causing conflict and disease

The disproportionate use of fresh water by tourists in developing world destinations is causing local conflict, exacerbating poverty and helping to spread disease, says a report to be published next week by the charity Tourism Concern.

"While hotels may have the money and resources to ensure their guests enjoy several showers a day, swimming pools, a round of golf, and lush landscaped gardens, neighbouring households, small businesses and agricultural producers can regularly endure severe water scarcity," says the report.

In the resort villages of Kiwengwa and Nungwi in Zanzibar, Tourism Concern's researchers found that, on average, tourists were using 16 times more fresh water a day per head than locals. The researchers found that locals used, on average, 93.2 litres of water per day, whereas in the five-star hotels the average daily consumption per room was 3,195 litres. In less luxurious tourist "guesthouses", the consumption rate fell to 686 litres per day.

The water crisis has led some Zanzibar hotels to employ security guards to protect the water pipes leading into their walled complexes following sabotage attempts by angry locals who claim they are facing extreme shortages as a result of the area's falling water table. "Hoteliers were taking much water and communities decided to demonstrate and destroy the water system to the hotels," one Nungwi villager told a Tourism Concern researcher.

In 2010, an outbreak of cholera in the Zanzibar resort village of Jambiani, which killed three locals, was blamed, in part, on sewage from hotels contaminating ground water.

Tourism Concern is calling on the international tourism industry, destination governments and tourists to urgently address this problem of "massive inequality".

Leo Hickman
Guardian.co.uk, Sunday 8 July 2012

Text 4

It is lonely at the lands where the people go to plough. These lands are vast clearings in the bush, and the wild bush is lonely too. Nearly all the lands are within walking distance from the village. In some parts of the bush where the underground water is very near the surface, people made little rest camps for themselves and dug shallow wells to quench their thirst while on their journey to their own lands. They experienced all kinds of things once they left the village. They could rest at shady watering places full of lush tangled trees with delicate pale-gold and purple wild flowers springing up between soft green moss and the children could hunt around for wild figs and any berries that might be in season. But from 1958, a seven-year drought fell upon the land and even the watering places began to look as dismal as the dry open thorn-bush country; the leaves of the trees curled up and withered; the moss became dry and hard and, under the shade of the tangled trees, the ground turned a powdery black and white, because there was no rain. People said rather humorously that if you tried to catch the rain in a cup it would only fill a teaspoon. Towards the beginning of the seventh year of drought, the summer had become an anguish to live through. The air was so dry and moisture-free that it burned the skin. No one knew what to do to escape the heat and tragedy was in the air. At the beginning of that summer, a number of men just went out of their homes and hung themselves to death from trees. The majority of the people had lived off crops, but for two years past they had all returned from the lands with only their rolled-up skin blankets and cooking utensils. Only the charlatans, incanters, and witch-doctors made a pile of money during this time because people were always turning to them in desperation for little talismans and herbs to rub on the plough for the crops to grow and the rain to fall.

The rains were late that year. They came in early November, with a promise of good rain. It wasn't the full, steady downpour of the years of good rain, but thin, scanty, misty rain. It softened the earth and a rich growth of green things sprang up everywhere for the animals to eat. People were called to the village kgotla to hear the proclamation of the beginning of the ploughing season; they stirred themselves and whole families began to move off to the lands to plough.

From short story: *Looking for a Rain God*
Bessie Head (1995)

Sample paper one: higher level

Choose either Section A or Section B

Section A

Analyse, compare and contrast the following two texts. Include comments on the similarities and differences between the two texts and the significance of context, purpose, and formal and stylistic features.

Text 1

Mumbai's Shadow City

Some call the Dharavi slum an embarrassing eyesore in the middle of India's financial capital. Its residents call it home.

All cities in India are loud, but nothing matches the 24/7 decibel level of Mumbai, the former Bombay, where the traffic never stops and the horns always honk. Noise, however, is not a problem in Dharavi, the teeming slum of one million souls, where as many as 18,000 people crowd into a single acre (0.4 hectares). By nightfall, deep inside the maze of lanes too narrow even for the putt-putt of auto rickshaws, the slum is as still as a verdant glade. Once you get accustomed to sharing 300 square feet (28 square meters) of floor with 15 humans and an uncounted number of mice, a strange sense of relaxation sets in—ah, at last a moment to think straight.

Ask any long time resident—some families have been here for three or more generations—how Dharavi came to be, and they'll say, "We built it." This is not far off. Until the late 19th century, this area of Mumbai was mangrove swamp inhabited by Koli fishermen. When the swamp filled in (with coconut leaves, rotten fish, and human waste), the Kolis were deprived of their fishing grounds—they would soon shift to bootlegging liquor—but room became available for others. The Kumbhars came from Gujarat to establish a potters' colony. Tamils arrived from the south and opened tanneries. Thousands travelled from Uttar Pradesh to work in the booming textile industry. The result is the most diverse of slums, arguably the most diverse neighbourhood in Mumbai, India's most diverse city.

Stay for a while on the three-foot-wide (one meter) lane of Rajendra Prasad Chawl, and you become acquainted with the rhythms of the place. The morning sound of devotional singing is followed by the rush of water. Until recently few people in Dharavi had water hookups. Residents such as Meera Singh, a wry woman who has lived on the lane for 35 years, used to walk a mile (two kilometers) to get water for the day's cleaning and cooking. At the distant spigot she would have to pay the local "goons" to fill her buckets. This is how it works in the bureaucratic twilight zone of informal housing. Deprived of public services because of their illegal status, slum dwellers often find themselves at the mercy of the "land mafia." There are water goons, electricity goons. In this regard, the residents of Rajendra Prasad Chawl are fortunate. These days, by DIY hook or crook, nearly every household on the street has its own water tap. And today, like every day, residents open their hoses to wash down the lane as they stand in the doorways of their homes to brush their teeth.

By Mark Jacobson, National Geographic Online Magazine, May 2007

Text 2

Blessing

The skin cracks like a pod.
There is never enough water.

Imagine the drip of it,
the small splash, echo
in a tin mug,
the voice of a kindly god.

Sometimes, the sudden rush
of fortune. The municipal pipe bursts,
silver crashes to the ground
and the flow has found
a roar of tongues. From the huts,
a congregation: every man woman
child for streets around
butts in, with pots,
brass, copper, aluminium,
plastic buckets,
frantic hands,

and naked children
screaming in the liquid sun,
their highlights polished to perfection,
flashing light,
as the blessing sings
over their small bones.

Imtiaz Dharker (1954-)

Blessing was published in Dharker's first book of poetry *Purdah* in 1989

Text 3

It was shocking to hear army trucks rumbling through the streets of my little town and to see men in green uniforms leaning against the walls of my friends' houses. Wau was not my simple home any longer; it was a military zone, with rebels on the outskirts, soldiers in town and the lawless militias wreaking havoc everywhere. I couldn't even climb the hill to spot planes anymore, because the soldiers had communications equipment up there and they'd be suspicious of what a young Dinka girl was doing.

For several months only military flights had been allowed to land at the airport so I'd known that a lot of soldiers were coming into the area. They'd kept pretty much to themselves and I'd hardly seen them on the streets. Now I couldn't walk to school without passing lots of guns, and even tanks. I marvelled at the machinery. It was hard to imagine they could turn it on me, but when my mother told us never to dawdle on the streets because they were just too dangerous I began to realise that the soldiers weren't necessarily there to protect me. My parents definitely didn't allow us out after dark.

However, we tried to keep our daily activities up. My mother would still take the cows to pasture and there was always water to bring home from the pump. One afternoon my younger sister Athieng and I put our plastic water containers on our heads and went to fetch water. We saw some other children there and we started playing hide-and-seek. I loved hanging out with Athieng because, unlike my other siblings, she didn't boss me around. She actually looked up to me. I was in my favourite hiding place, behind a fat old acacia tree – for some reason everyone always forgot to look there.

After a while we paused for a drink of water. Suddenly the daylight turned that deep yellow colour you only see on the equator and I realised that twilight was descending. Mother would be worried.

'We've got to get home,' I said, grabbing Athieng's arm. We filled the canisters and rushed off, droplets falling onto our faces as we hadn't closed the lids properly. I made sure my sister kept her eyes on the path whenever we met someone on the way home. The darkness always made the militias hungry for stealing and shooting. I wasn't going to let anyone hurt my sister. A green military half-track passed, kicking up red dust. One of the soldiers in camouflage peered at me from below his dark beret. His teeth were white and he licked his dry lips as he watched us. We ran back along the road, passing more green trucks on the way. Helmets, guns and gas canisters hung from the sides of the trucks and the soldiers looked primed, excited, ready for action. It scared the life out of me. My sister and I ran into our courtyard and hurriedly closed the gate, trying to keep the world out.

There were our mother's cows, her vegetables. It felt good to be home. Inside, my mother and father were hunched over the radio, listening at low volume. My mother looked up, held her finger in front of her mouth and said, 'Shhhh – close the door.' They were listening to the rebel radio station, which was illegal. You didn't want anyone to catch you listening to it. On the radio the announcer was saying that the conflict had spread to Wau.

'War?' I said.

My father nodded. The war had resumed, after ten years of peace. They'd been keeping it from us children, hoping that it would bypass Wau. But now it was too late for that.

Text 4

Teenagers 'harden views on immigration as they age'

Most 18-year-olds believe new arrivals should be forced to learn English, study by National Foundation for Education Research finds

English teenagers become increasingly intolerant of immigrants and refugees as they grow older, and hold notably harder views on the issue than their counterparts in other countries, according to a pair of mass-participation studies released today.

The first survey tracked the attitudes of more than 24,000 English school pupils between the ages of 11 and 18. It found that the young people "become less tolerant in practice towards equality and society" over the period of the study – 2002 to 2009 – with their attitudes becoming less sympathetic not only towards refugees and immigrants, but also over jail sentences and benefit payments.

The survey was carried out by the National Foundation for Education Research (NFER) charity, which also took part in the separate poll of 14-year-olds in 38 countries, 24 of them in Europe. This found that while pupils in England, 3,500 of whom were polled, held "broadly democratic and tolerant" attitudes, their tolerance of immigration was notably below the international average, with particular opposition towards migration from within Europe.

"It's interesting in that we have these two studies – the longitudinal study from 11 to 18 and the snapshot at the age of 14 – and they seem to be saying similar things," said Professor David Kerr from the NFER. "They support notions of equality in gender and race in theory, but when it comes to actual immigration, they are less tolerant than young people in the other countries. It could be that we're living in an increasingly competitive world and they are mainly worried for their own prospects."

Almost 80% of the 18-year-olds said British residents not born in the country should be compelled to learn English, against half who believed this at 11.

They were also found to participate increasingly in charity and community activities, although many admitted doing so more out of hope of personal advancement than civic duty.

The separate worldwide study found the English pupils had an interest in news media "significantly below the international average", as well as low confidence in their ability to influence political issues.

Perhaps unsurprisingly, the global study found English pupils had significantly less knowledge of the EU than their European peers. They expressed a degree of European identity but viewed themselves as primarily British.

Peter Walker, The Guardian, Monday 22 November 2010

Write an analysis on one of the following texts. Include comments on the significance of context, audience, purpose, and formal and stylistic features.

Text 1

My year in disaster zones

When a disaster strikes or conflict breaks out, MSF emergency teams are often the first on the scene. Here, emergency coordinator and water sanitation expert HENRY GRAY looks back on a year of emergencies.

"When I arrived in Haiti during the cholera outbreak, I turned up at the hospital and looked around and thought, "Where on earth do I start?" There were people lying on the floor, bodies everywhere – it was terrible.

It's very easy to feel overwhelmed in situations like that, but you have to put that aside and make a start. Cholera demands a rapid response, and that's what we were there to do.

Working for MSF, you know that there will be people working around the clock making sure that supplies will be on the next flight. By week four or five, the deaths in our cholera treatment centres were much lower, as more people were getting the messages about the disease and the staff we had trained began to do more of the work. It was a terrible situation, but we were able to help people who needed help.

"In Haiti, I thought "Where on earth do I start?" There were bodies lying everywhere."

In April I was on a fishing boat being smuggled into Misrata in Libya. The city was under siege and being shelled daily. We knew there were medical needs there and had a team on the ground for a few months. The atmosphere was very tense. At night you'd often be woken with the cry of "Take cover!" You'd roll to your safe place, wait for the shelling to stop, and then try and go back to sleep.

My job there was to help get the water treatment plant working properly again. With our support the Libyan guys running the plant were able to produce 100 million litres a day of chlorinated water. That was extremely satisfying and well received.

Henry Gray, MSF emergency coordinator and water and sanitation expert.

£: YOUR SUPPORT
£48.36 a month or £580.32 will pay for an emergency medical kit with which we can provide 1000 people with medical care for 3 months.

MSF appeal supplement, The Observer (2012)

113

Text 2

In a quarter of a century of globe-trotting, Michael Palin had never visited Brazil. Now he's put that right with a new TV series about the country. Here he reveals his highlights and, right, we explain how to follow in his footsteps

For a long time I thought of Brazil as a state of mind. A fantasy of sun, sea, samba and lots of other words beginning with "s". I partly blame Terry Gilliam, for in Brazil, his 1985 film, he uses the lilting samba beat of the eponymous song (known as Aquarela do Brasil in its native land) to accompany the final crushing of his hero by the mad, dysfunctional world around him. The song represents pure unproductive pleasure. Brazil as the ultimate escapist image.

The Latin American mind-set is one with which we north Europeans can't easily identify. China we can relate to because it's single-minded and industrious; India and the sub-continent is crazy and colourful and quite a bit English. Russia is dark and impenetrable but good at putting up with things, which we admire. The Brazilians on the other hand don't have to put up with anything. They have everything. Spicy seafood stews, fruits of the forest and luscious caipirinhas. Swaying music, sensual dancers and perfect bodies, wrapped in balmy warmth and enveloped in rapturous sex. As they say, what's not to like. Even as we read about drug gangs and watch violent films such as City of God, we give Brazil the benefit of the doubt. Bound to be some bad 'uns in a country that plays such beautiful football.

So, for me, Brazil's mystique grew, hot and steamy and lush as the jungles that I assumed to cover most of the country. Even its location seemed a touch other-worldly. Most of it in the southern hemisphere and not exactly on the way to anywhere, except possibly Peru or Paraguay. My early attempts to learn more about it only strengthened the mythology. Brazil's northern border was the setting of Conan Doyle's Lost World. The explorer Colonel Percy Fawcett who went deep into the rainforest to discover El Dorado, was never seen again. Peter Fleming, who went to find him, got lost too and just got out of the jungle alive. (Brazilian Adventure, Fleming's first book, is nevertheless, one of the funniest books about nearly dying.)

The Guardian travel supplement (20 October 2012)

Sample paper one: standard level

Write an analysis on one of the following texts. Include comments on the significance of context, audience, purpose, and formal and stylistic features.

Text 1

April 15th, Thursday. It was a threatening, misty morning, but mild. We set off after dinner from Eusemere. Mrs Clarkson went a short way with us, but turned back. The wind was furious, and we thought we must have returned. We first rested in the large Boat-house, then under a furze bush opposite Mr Clarkson's. Saw the plough going in the field. The wind seized our breath. The lake was rough. There was a Boat floating by itself in the middle of the Bay below Water Millock. We rested again in the Water Millock Lane. The hawthorns are black and green, the birches here and there greenish, but there is yet more of purple to be seen on the twigs. We got over into a field to avoid some cows—people working. A few primroses by the roadside - woodsorrel flower, the anemone, scentless violets, strawberries, and that starry, yellow flower which Mrs. C. Calls pile wort. When we were in the woods beyond Gowbarrow park we saw a few daffodils close to the water-side. We fancied that the lake had floated the seeds ashore, and that the little colony had so sprung up. But as we went along there were more and yet more; and at last, under the boughs of the trees, we saw that there was a long belt of them along the shore, about the breadth of a country turn-pike road. I never saw daffodils so beautiful. They grew among the mossy stones about and about them; some rested their heads upon these stones as on a pillow for weariness; and the rest tossed and reeled and danced, and seemed as if they verily laughed with the wind, that blew upon them over the lake; they looked so gay, ever glancing, ever changing. This wind blew directly over the lake to them. There was here and there a little knot, and a few stragglers a few yards higher up; but they were so few as not to disturb the simplicity, unity, and life of that one busy highway. We rested again and again. The bays were stormy, and we heard the waves at different distances, and in the middle of the water, like the sea.

Extract from **Dorothy Wordsworth's Diary**

Text 2

One day soon, somewhere deep in a rainforest in South America or Borneo or Central Africa, a few nervous men and women will step into a muddy clearing in the jungle. Cautiously, they will accept the steel machetes or cooking pots being held out by a government-sponsored anthropologist, before hurrying back into the safety of the forest.

The encounter will not be marked by any great fanfare. It will probably not make the news. Yet it will be a significant landmark in human history. The last 'uncontacted' tribe on earth will have been caught in our global web, and an era of exploration, invasion and global integration that began when Columbus first set eyes on the Americas will be over. For the first time, the entire human race will be connected in one giant, all-embracing cultural and trading network.

As this era of human history comes to a close, we are left with a dominant social and economic system that ignores human and environmental costs. A system that destroys communal life because of its demand for a mobile labour force. That creates mental illnesses and stress by sucking people into huge, anonymous cities. That discourages people from growing their own food because doing so doesn't involve selling anything (and therefore doesn't show up as profit in economic statistics). A system that puts a greater value on a pile of dead wood than on a living forest.

Beginning with the triangular colonial trade in slaves and sugar, a Western-dominated global economy has imposed itself on the world. This is the so-called 'free market': imposed by deceit and force, from the brutality of the conquistadors and the gunboat diplomacy of the British Empire to CIA-backed coups and the financial bullying of the International Monetary Fund.

The engine that drives the system is trade. Almost all human societies have engaged in some form of trade, but the global economy is unique in its scope and the way it aggressively destroys local self-sufficiency and replaces it with global trade relationships that defy common sense. These are trade relationships in which an apple transported half-way around the world via a massive infrastructure of expensive planes, airports, trucks and roads can still cost less that the same apple grown a few miles from your home.

From *The Community Tourism Guide: Exciting Holidays for Responsible Travellers*
Mark Mann (2000)

IBDP REVISION COURSES

Summary

Who are they for?
Students about to take their final IBDP exams (May or November)

Locations include:
Oxford, UK
Rome, Italy
Brussels, Belgium
Dubai, UAE
Adelaide, Sydney & Melbourne, AUS
Munich, Germany

Duration
2.5 days per subject
Students can take multiple subjects

The most successful IB revision courses worldwide

Highly-experienced IB teachers and examiners

Every class is tailored to the needs of that particular group of students

Features

- Classes grouped by grade (UK)
- Exam skills and techniques – typical traps identified
- Exam practice
- Pre-course online questionnaire to identify problem areas
- Small groups of 8–10 students
- 24-hour pastoral care.

Revising for the final IB exams without expert guidance is tough. Students attending OSC Revision Courses get more work done in a shorter time than they could possibly have imagined.

With a different teacher, who is confident in their subject and uses their experience and expertise to explain new approaches and exam techniques, students rapidly improve their understanding. OSC's teaching team consists of examiners and teachers with years of experience – they have the knowledge and skills students need to get top grades.

The size of our Oxford course gives some particular advantages to students. With over 1,000 students and 300 classes, we can group students by grade – enabling them to go at a pace that suits them.

Students work hard, make friends and leave OSC feeling invigorated and confident about their final exams.

We understand the needs of IBDP students – our decades of experience, hand-picked teachers and intense atmosphere can improve your grades.

"I got 40 points overall, two points up from my prediction of 38, and up 7 points from what I had been scoring in my mocks over the years, before coming to OSC. Thank you so much for all your help!

OSC Student

Please note that locations and course features are subject to change - please check our website for up-to-date details.

Find out more: 🏠 osc-ib.com/revision 📱 +44 (0)1865 512802

MID IBDP SUMMER PROGRAMMES

Summary

Who is it for?
For students entering their final year of the IB Diploma Programme

Locations include:
Harvard and MIT, USA
Cambridge, UK

Duration
Min. 1 week, max. 6 weeks
1 or 2 IB subjects per week

Improve confidence and grades

Highly-experienced IB teachers and examiners

Tailored classes to meet students' needs

Wide range of available subjects

Safe accommodation and 24-hour pastoral care

Features

- Morning teaching in chosen IB subject
- 2nd IB subject afternoon classes
- IB Skills afternoon classes
- One-to-one Extended Essay Advice, Private Tuition and University Guidance options
- Small classes
- Daily homework
- Unique IB university fair
- Class reports for parents
- Full social programme.

By the end of their first year, students understand the stimulating and challenging nature of the IB Diploma.

They also know that the second year is crucial in securing the required grades to get into their dream college or university.

This course helps students to avoid a 'summer dip' by using their time effectively. With highly-experienced IB teachers, we consolidate a student's year one learning, close knowledge gaps, and introduce some year two material.

In a relaxed environment, students develop academically through practice revision and review. They are taught new skills, techniques, and perspectives – giving a real boost to their grades. This gives students an enormous amount of confidence and drive for their second year.

The whole experience was incredible. The university setting was inspiring, the friends I made, and the teaching was first-class. I feel so much more confident in myself and in my subject.

OSC Student

Please note that locations and course features are subject to change - please check our website for up-to-date details.

Find out more: osc-ib.com/mid   +44 (0)1865 512802